The Story of the Jewish Legion
by Vladimir Jabotinsky

Vladimir Jabotinsky

The Story of The Jewish Legion

TRANSLATED BY

Samuel Katz

WITH A FOREWORD BY

Col. John Henry Patterson, D.S.O.

AND AN AFTERWORD BY

Prof. Benzion Netanyahu

The Toby Press

The Story of the Jewish Legion
by Vladimir Jabotinsky

Koren Publishers Jerusalem is honored to publish this
Second English Edition of '*The Story of the Jewish Legion*'
in cooperation with The Jabotinsky Institute.

Managing Editor: Uri Bollag
Editing: Rachel Miskin, Ruth Pepperman
Cover Design: Tani Bayer
Typesetting: Tomi Mager

POB 8531, New Milford, CT 06776–8531, USA
& POB 4044, Jerusalem 9104001, Israel

ISBN 978–1-59264–747–7, *hardcover*
ISBN 978–1-59264–753–8, *paperback*

Printed and bound in Israel

Contents

Foreword

John Henry Patterson

I

Vladimir Jabotinsky's last walk on earth was between two lines of young Betarim, who awaited his arrival in Camp Betar in Hunter, New York. They stood in military formation for his inspection. Although suffering from acute pain, Jabotinsky carried out the inspection and went straight to his room and died – a martyr to duty even unto death.

I was not with him during the last hours of his life, but when I later heard of it I could not help saying to myself that if Jabotinsky were to choose the setting for his death, it would have been something after this manner. The inspection of a Betar parade as his last deed in this world was highly symbolical.

Not that Jabotinsky was a born soldier. He was not. Not only by my standards – the standards of a man who has spent many years of his life in army service – but by any standard, Jabotinsky was of course a "civilian." While in the Jewish Legion, he made an excellent soldier; as fine and brave, as disciplined and courageous as any. However, no one who knew the man at all could possibly have missed those exceptional gifts of statesmanship, intellect, leadership and oratory with which he was endowed in such unparalleled abundance. It was too wonderful a combination to be restricted by any army uniform. If there had existed a Republic of Israel, Jabotinsky would have made an ideal president. But there was neither a Jewish Republic nor a Jewish Army, except for the Legion in World War I, which came into being primarily through Jabotinsky's vision and his stubborn determination not to rest until the Legion became a reality.

Yet, maybe for the very reason that the Jews had no army of their own and the Jewish Legion was a comparatively short-lived affair; maybe because the Legion remained Jabotinsky's most outstanding success, the most brilliant page in the history of his crowded life, the "civilian" Jabotinsky never lost his military bearing.

He was thirty-six years old when he joined the Jewish Legion, having spent all his life prior to that either at the desk writing his books, articles and poems, or on the platforms all over Russia trying to imbue Jewry with the Zionist idea. After about two years of military schooling and service, he once again returned to the very active life of a political writer, lecturer, propagandist and leader of his people. Only two years in the army as against forty years of civilian endeavors, but no one who came in contact with the man could have been in any doubt as to his military past. It was not only Jabotinsky's upright, soldier-like bearing, which he maintained with inborn ease all through the years to the last day of his life, but it seemed to me that Jabotinsky found in the army a response to his innermost longings, something he badly wanted, maybe not so much for himself as for his people.

Jabotinsky used to say of himself, as he mentions also in this book, that he had a "*Goyishe kop*." By that he meant that his mentality was fundamentally the mentality of a Christian, void of the peculiar inhibitions of a Jewish mind influenced and twisted by the abnormalities of centuries of life in dispersion. As a Christian I venture to say that by describing himself as a "*Goyishe kop*," Jabotinsky badly belittled his mental capacities. His scholarly mind, his broad erudition, his exceptional linguistic abilities and the brilliance which loomed out of every word he spoke or wrote were not "*Goyish*" but Jewish. It took generations of Jewish scholars and rabbis, of Jewish suffering and Jewish idealism to produce a Vladimir Jabotinsky. Still, there *was* something in him of the "*Goyishe kop*." Jabotinsky the Jewish statesman was predominantly a "*Goyishe kop*." That was probably the main reason why his political philosophy was so healthy and simple, and why with all his tremendous popularity he never became the recognized leader of the Jewish people.

It took me many years of close friendship with Jabotinsky and of comradely collaboration in many ventures, before I began to understand where the Jew in him ended and the "*Goy*" began. But not until I read *Prelude to Delilah,* the biblical novel about Samson in which Jabotinsky puts on Samson's lips a great deal of his political philosophy, could I draw myself a full picture of Jabotinsky's make-up. I shall later return to *Prelude to Delilah,* but at this stage I would venture this rough definition: Jabotinsky's spirit was Jewish; his way of thinking was "*Goyish*."

According to the account of his conversation with Max Nordau, reproduced in this book, Nordau said to Jabotinsky: "That, my young friend, is logic. But logic is a Greek art which the Jews hate." That is it! Jabotinsky's logic was non-Jewish, and logic – logic alone – played the overwhelming part in his political thinking and actions.

There was a widespread conception of Jabotinsky as a man led by emotions, a man of uncontrollable enthusiasms. His great oratory, which often enthused beyond control great multitudes of people, contributed to the formation of this misconception of Jabotinsky. For a gross misconception it was. One could rarely meet a man with whom emotions would carry so little weight in his political thinking and actions. Indeed, in the numerous encounters with statesmen of many lands which I have had, I cannot recall one who was as much a slave of his logic as Jabotinsky was. One of the most colorful, experienced and magnetic orators of his day, Jabotinsky would never mount a platform without first preparing carefully his lecture or speech up to the last of his studied gestures. He would leave nothing to chance, and he did not believe in miracles. In logic he believed, in the logic of mankind, in the logic of events and in the logic which must rule supremely in our lives. This was the most striking non-Jewish feature in his mentality. There was practically no bridge between Jabotinsky's logic and the Jewish submissiveness to chance, miracle and fate.

When on that rainy morning in 1914 he read the news of Turkey's entry into the war, he arrived by way of sound reasoning at the idea of a Jewish Legion. The way he tells it in this book, it was all very simple, an obvious logical conclusion to be arrived at by any Jewish intelligent observer of world affairs. That that implied no less than a revolution in the history of the Jewish dispersion and in the Jewish political philosophy of the last two thousand years was a minor consideration, as compared with the supreme demands of sound logic. Only later, when confronted with the bitter and determined opposition to the Legion idea not only of diehard assimilationists but of organized Zionism, did Jabotinsky probably recall the wise words of Max Nordau that "logic is a Greek art which the Jews hate." Did this discourage him or stop his efforts to form a Jewish Legion, boycotted by many Jews among them the leading Zionists, cold-shouldered by the Allied statesmen, actively opposed by so many and supported by so few? Well, logic might be a Greek art, and Jabotinsky was a Jew, but it certainly was his, Jabotinsky's, *alpha* and *omega* of political thinking.

In 1937, Jabotinsky was on a campaign tour in South Africa. In April, one of his colleagues at the New Zionist Headquarters in London went out to join him in Johannesburg. Of the news he brought from London, the most important item was a report of the forthcoming plan of the Royal Commission for the partition of Palestine. He told Jabotinsky the story with a very worried air. Jabotinsky asked for details, pondered over them for a little while, and then turned to his colleague smilingly: "Wipe the worry off your face. The whole plan does not stand to reason and it will never become a reality." It does not stand to reason, and that is all there is to it.

When, in 1933, the tragic news came from Palestine of the murder of Dr. Arlozoroff on the beach of Tel Aviv and the subsequent arrest of two Revisionists accused of the murder, Jabotinsky did not fly off on a tangent in some emotional outburst. He studied minutely all the reports, as he later followed from afar the court proceedings; he analyzed dispassionately all the facts of the situation, and only when he arrived at the conclusion that "it does not stand to reason," he threw himself unreservedly into a campaign to save the two innocent young men and to smash the false accusation against them.

Logic, the Greek art, was Jabotinsky's guide in political thinking. That is why he felt more deeply than anyone else the abnormalities of Jewish political society. That is why he longed so badly for a state organization for his people, for an army, discipline and the overall normalcy which every other nation possesses. In his novel, *Prelude to Delilah*, Jabotinsky gives expression to his political philosophy to a greater extent than in his many articles dealing with current problems. There, in the life of Samson, in the riddles which he used to pose to the Philistines and in his wise aphorisms, Jabotinsky states his innermost dreams and longings. When I read this book years ago, I finally understood what it was that Jabotinsky searched for in the Jewish Legion, and what it was that made of this short episode a lasting imprint on his life.

One could quote endlessly from *Prelude to Delilah* in elucidation of Jabotinsky's way of thinking. Indeed, whoever wants to understand Jabotinsky must read that enlightening book. But I shall quote only one passage, which will suffice for what I wish to bring out. It is a passage from one of the last chapters. The heroic days of Samson were already ended. He had been seized by the Philistines, blinded by them, and was living in captivity in the humblest quarter of Gaza. From time to time people came from Judea, asking him to come back to his own people, but he constantly refused. One day, one of his close followers and admirers, Hermesh, came on the same mission and got the same reply. Before leaving, Hermesh asked Samson whether he had a message for his people, and this was the message of Samson:

"Tell them two things in my name – two words. The first word is Iron. They must get iron. They must give everything they have for iron – their silver and wheat, oil and wine and flocks, even their wives and daughters. All for iron! There is nothing in the world more valuable than iron. Will you tell them that?"

"I will. They will understand that."

"The second word they will not understand yet, but they must learn to understand it, and that soon. The second word is this: A King! Say to Dan, Benjamin, Judah, Ephraim: a king! A man will give them the signal and of a sudden thousands will lift up their hands. So it is with the Philistines, and therefore the Philistines are lords of Canaan. Say it from Zorah to Hebron and Shechem, and farther even to Endor and Laish: a king!"

Here is what Jabotinsky looked for in the Jewish Legion and what drove him to a Jewish state: "Iron and a King." In these two short words you can find everything: Jabotinsky's uncompromising revolt against the unorganized, formless Jewish dispersion with no state organization, no leadership, no discipline and no national policy. And you can find in it, too, the foundations of his simple yet sound and constructive political program for the Jewish people. He wanted for the Jews what they lacked most: a united nation with a central leadership; a state with an army; "iron" for their defense in a hostile world, and a man who gives the signal and thousands lift up their hands....

That is why it was he, Jabotinsky, who originated the idea of a Jewish Legion in World War I, and fought for a Jewish Army in World War II. This it was that prompted him to organize Jewish self-defense back in Russia and later in Palestine. This was behind his idea of the Brit Trumpeldor movement, which he loved and cherished more than any other of his creations. In these Betar youngsters he was hoping to arouse the great longing for "Iron and King," for military preparedness, organization, self-respect and discipline – all those elements of nationhood which he so badly missed in Jewish life, and which, he knew, were the indispensable foundations for the rebirth of Jewish statehood.

II

If one lacks historic perspective and the knowledge of the specific conditions of Jewish life, one can hardly appreciate the titanic role played by Jabotinsky in the creation of the Jewish Legion in World War I. Indeed now, in the days of World War II, the Jewish Legion may seem to some people as something insignificant and hardly worth talking about. Are not there "armies in exile" of the Poles, Czechs, French and others in this war? What is there so important about a Jewish Legion of a few thousand men fighting in the British Army in the last war? Only after consideration of all the circumstances of the case can one arrive at a realistic evaluation of the feat of Jabotinsky.

When Jabotinsky embarked on the Jewish Legion venture, everything was against him and there was nothing whatever to give support to his idea. First of all, it was a precedent-breaking idea. Since the fall of Judea and the Jewish dispersion all over the globe, there never was a Jewish military unit anywhere in the world. For two thousand years, the Jews had had neither a state organization of their own nor any military formation of their own. Furthermore, by the very fact of the Jewish dispersion, the Jewish people had a stake in every land, and this was later to be one of the chief arguments of the opponents of the Jewish Legion. "How can we dare," they would say, "to join either of the warring alliances, thus endangering the Jewish populations of the other alliance?" In other words, they claimed that if a Jewish Legion was formed within the framework of the British Army, the Jews of Germany, Austria, Bulgaria and Turkey would pay the price, for surely vengeance would engulf them.

This in itself was no idle argument, for Jewish realities demanded consideration. Jewish minorities lived everywhere, practically at the mercy of the ruling majorities. But even more powerful was the unspoken argument of a long-lasting tradition, of the very philosophy of the Jewish *Galut* (Dispersion).

In most countries of Europe, especially in Eastern, Central and Southern Europe, where the bulk of the Jewish people lived, the Jews were neither *de jure* nor *de facto* full-fledged citizens of their respective states. Also in spirit, moreover, they did not feel like full-fledged members of these European nations. This state of affairs, which developed during several centuries, had brought about a widespread indifference among the Jews regarding the fate of such states. They were not expected to be wholehearted patriots of the countries which treated them like stepchildren – and they were no such patriots, though to the extent they were allowed to serve such countries they always served them loyally. What they principally were concerned with – for very obvious reasons – was how this or that development in the nations among whom they lived as a hated or persecuted minority would affect their own lives and interests.

Step by step, this attitude, logical and justified as it was in light of the treatment accorded to the Jews in all those countries, developed into a kind of philosophy of the Jewish *Galut*. It was a philosophy of complete passivism. The Jewish mind has provided an ideological foundation for the sad realities of their life. The Jews have become an object in the play of forces in history, but for the present at least, not a subject taking an active part in the march of history. A pogrom in Russia or Rumania, an antisemitic outburst in Germany, a Dreyfus affair in France, or wars between the various nations of Europe were to be considered as major or minor holocausts, from which one had to escape but which one could not actively combat. Fate, which has taken care of Israel for so many centuries, would somehow save Israel again, but what could Israel himself do?...

It is against this background of thorough passivism consecrated by hundreds of years of tradition that Jabotinsky's idea of a Jewish Legion has to be seen, in order to realize the depth of the abyss which divided Jabotinsky's way of thinking from that of Jewry as a whole. Indeed, if he were to have called the Jews to take up arms in order to defend themselves from an attack by local hooligans or pogromists – as he did in his earlier days in Russia and later in Palestine – his appeal would have fallen on much more receptive ears. But what he wanted this time was an official emergence of the Jewish people from the traditional state of absolute neutrality in a war among the European nations. He wanted to transform the Jewish people from a conglomeration of minorities living in various lands and officially belonging to the various nations, into a nation of its own with a national policy of its own. Small as the Jewish Legion was in number, it was to be a symbol of a Jewish Army, and what is more: an official proclamation of belligerency on behalf of the Jewish people as such. No more neutrality, no more passivism, but a very active stand of a co-ally with the Allies. If there ever was a call for a national revolution, Jabotinsky's idea of a Jewish Legion was such a call. It was a revolution against tradition, against the fundamental way of thinking of his people, and a call to take a national stand in world events.

No wonder that Jabotinsky encountered such fierce opposition among Jewry to his idea of a Legion. The wonder was that he found in himself enough strength to go on with his campaign for a Jewish Legion despite that opposition, and to bring it to ultimate realization. For Jabotinsky had to overcome not only the internal Jewish antagonism to his proposal, but also innumerable obstacles on the external front. It would be difficult to assess now which of the oppositions, the Jewish one or that of the world at large, was more formidable, but it is safe to state that he had to swim against powerful currents.

The appreciation of the enormous difficulties which Jabotinsky had to overcome among Jewry did not come to me all at once. When I was appointed, first to the command of the Zion Mule Corps in Gallipoli, and then to that of the Jewish Legion, I knew as little of contemporary Jewry, its conditions of life and its peculiar problems, as any Englishman. Only after my close association with the Jewish Legion and Vladimir Jabotinsky, which resulted in my lively interest in Jewish affairs in the ensuing years, did this picture develop before my eyes in all its implications. That part of Jabotinsky's battle for the Legion I realized in retrospect. But his fight in the international political sphere passed before my eyes. Furthermore, there I could judge as well as anyone what the reaction would be, and I knew that in diplomatic and military circles of England and of other European lands, Jabotinsky's idea of a Jewish Legion would be accorded anything but an enthusiastic reception.

Another thirty years had to pass before the world would get accustomed to kings and governments living and acting in exile while their countries were occupied by the enemy. Governments in exile and armies in exile were unknown in 1914. Even less chance of understanding and acceptance stood the idea of an army of a people which had no national territory of its own. For world political thought, Jabotinsky's idea of a Jewish Legion was not simply precedent-breaking, it was contrary to all precedents. It is true that he did not advocate at that time the formation of an independent Jewish army, but only of Jewish regiments in the British Army (later he tried to do the same in France and failed). Nevertheless, those were to be Jewish regiments. From a purely British point of view, it only added to difficulties. The French had a Foreign Legion, which was a kind of haven for desperados, adventurers or exiles from all over the world. The British had no such formations. And it was not this kind of a foreign legion that Jabotinsky suggested, but a formation with a very definite national and political objective.

The fact that this unprecedented foreign formation in the British Army was to be *Jewish* did not help in any way. Today, after the experiences of the first and second World Wars, very few military experts have any doubts as to the fighting abilities, endurance, courage and intelligence of the Jewish soldier. Only confirmed antisemites whose anti-Jewish feelings are stronger than their judgment of facts, would refuse to admit that the contemporary Jew has proved himself to be among the best fighters in the world. We must remember, however, that back in 1914, there was no proof as to the stouthearted qualities of the Jew as a soldier, and absolutely no precedent on which a judgment could be formed.

People in the British Foreign Office and in the War Office saw before them a Jewish-Russian journalist with an idea. Why he wanted a Jewish Legion they could well guess, for they were aware of the Jewish-Zionist aspirations regarding Palestine. What, however, would be the practical value of Jewish regiments? What kind of fighters were the contemporary Jews? Would it be an asset or a liability to have Jewish military formations within the British Army? There was no one at that time who could answer those questions with any degree of certainty. This Jewish journalist from Russia looked a very determined fellow who knew exactly what he wanted, but the British officials were well aware of the widespread opposition to the Legion idea in Jewry itself, all the way from the Zionist headquarters to the poor Jewish masses of Whitechapel and the rich Jewish notables in the city. This was the atmosphere in which Jabotinsky had to fight for the materialization of the Jewish Legion. Besides the revolution in Jewry, he had to perform a revolution in the whole conception of Jewry in British minds.

III

That Jabotinsky succeeded in performing the two revolutions is now a matter of record. In this book he tells the story of the Jewish Legion, to which I may be able to add some of my own recollections.

Jabotinsky "builded better than he knew," when at Alexandria, Egypt, in the early days of 1915, he sowed the seeds of a Jewish military unit which resulted, in its first stage, in the formation of the Zion Mule Corps. Although Jabotinsky himself did not join the Corps, it was his promotion of the idea of a Jewish Legion that was primarily responsible for the creation of the first organized Jewish unit in World War I.

On the twenty-third day of March in that year, Grand Rabbi Raphael della Pergola, with great solemnity, administered the "oath of obedience" to the massed ranks of the men of Zion. The five hundred recruits with uplifted hands repeated the oath after the Grand

Rabbi, and "swore obedience to the officer commanding the Corps and to such officers as should be placed over them."

It was not until the second of April that we were able to secure a campsite at Wardian, a suburb of Alexandria, and there pitch our tents and begin "all out" training for the arduous duties ahead. I was fortunate in having the invaluable assistance of the gallant Captain Joseph Trumpeldor – of whom Jabotinsky writes so glowingly in this book – in preparing the men for immediate active service. None of us had any idea in those strenuous days that we should be in the firing line, several hundred miles away on the Gallipoli Peninsula, by the twenty-fifth of April, little over three weeks after we started training – surely a record in military history.

We were not only a transport corps but a fighting corps to boot, and every man was equipped and trained to take his place on the battlefront – where in the rough and tumble of trench warfare the men of Zion often came to grips with their old enemies, the Turks.

It is not my intention to go into details of the services rendered and the gallant deeds performed by the now famous Zion Corps during the entire period of the Gallipoli invasion. If the reader is interested in details, he can find them in *With the Zionists in Gallipoli* – a modest record written by me of events just as they happened.

I may, however, state that we won some of the highest military awards during the campaign and everybody from General Sir Ian Hamilton, the Commander-in-Chief, down to the private in the ranks of the British Army, gave us unstinted praise. In fact, "The Zion Mule Corps became indispensable in Gallipoli." These are not my words but those of Sidney Moseley, a representative of the War Office who witnessed the outstanding gallantry and devotion to duty exhibited day after day by the Zion men on the shell-swept and bloody shores of the Dardanelles.

Eventually, when the High Command decreed the evacuation of the peninsula, the hardy Zionists were among the last to take to the boats for Egypt. Yes, Jabotinsky had indeed "builded better than he knew," for when he later tackled the London War Office on the creation of the Jewish Legion, he found that a legend of Jewish gallantry in Gallipoli had taken root there and this lightened his task immensely. In fact, had it not been for the incredible stupidity of the "Old Men of Zion" who strenuously opposed Jabotinsky's endeavors, I am certain that a Jewish Army of at least one hundred thousand men would have been formed. This was what a high-ranking general at the War Office told me when I was sent for to take command of the "Jewish Regiment," as the Legion was at first named.

What a difference a Jewish Army in World War I would have made! It is difficult to state now with absolute certainty what the subsequent march of events would have been; few people possess prophetic powers. It seems, however, safe to say that the whole course of history, especially with regard to Palestine and the Jewish people, would have been totally different. The Jewish people would have gained Palestine, whether the British bureaucrats liked it or not; and a Jewish Palestine would have provided England with another Gibraltar – faithful to her unto death – at the Eastern end of the Mediterranean. If one bears in mind that in such a case the Jews would have had a state of their own and *ipso facto* the British would have been much stronger in the Middle East, one may doubt whether Hitler would have found it so easy to bring about World War II. Few people now doubt the enormous part played by the Jewish problem in Europe by enabling Hitler to sow dissension all over the continent and so climb to power in Germany and in Europe. The extreme vulnerability of British positions in the Middle East, accompanied by military and strategic weaknesses, were also important factors in the war.

Yes, if only Jabotinsky's urgent pleadings had been listened to and a Jewish Army had been created to fight alongside the Allies in the First World War, great evils would surely have been averted and the world would have been quite a different place today. But his opponents, who could not shed their ghetto fears, were too strong for him. Instead of a great Jewish Army, a mere Jewish Legion had to suffice, and even this the ghetto men sought to belittle. The truth of the old

Greek proverb was never better exemplified: "Those whom the Gods are about to destroy, they first smite with blindness."

But to come back to the story of the Jewish Legion. I was still in the hospital, recovering from the hardships and ills of the Gallipoli campaign, when I first met Vladimir Jabotinsky. He had called to see me with the object of getting my consent to take command of the "Jewish Regiment," the creation of which was announced in the *London Gazette* of August 23, 1917.

I was much impressed with Jabotinsky the man, and a friendship was begun that day which ended only with his lamented death nearly a quarter of a century later. We worked together, fought together, and stood foursquare together, facing all kinds of troubles during those long trying years. Never could one have a better comrade or a truer friend than Vladimir Jabotinsky.

It was a proud moment in the life of my friend when he was gazetted a lieutenant in the 38th Battalion of the Royal Fusiliers on the selfsame day that he carried a Jewish banner at the head of the Battalion on a triumphal march through the city of London on February 4, 1918. The band of the Coldstream Guards played a stirring march as the men with fixed bayonets proudly strode past the Mansion House, where the Lord Mayor, attended by many generals from the War Office, took the salute.

On the following day we embarked at Southampton for Cherbourg, France, and thence overland via Marseilles and Genoa to Taranto, where we took ship for Alexandria, arriving in Egypt on February 28, 1918. From the moment of debarkation it was made plain by the Army staff that our arrival was deeply resented. The anti-Jewish chief of staff, General Louis Jean Bols, did his best to destroy us, but failed miserably.

For the remarkable achievements of the Legion in the Holy Land I must refer those interested to my book, *With the Judeans in the Palestine Campaign*. There it will be found that the Legion did all that was asked of it, and when Allenby gave the order for the final advance that drove the Turks out of Palestine, Jewish troops held the extreme right flank of his army. The objective of the Jewish Legion was the capture of the Umm Esh Shert ford over the Jordan.

This vital crossing was strongly held by the Turks, but nothing could stop the Legionaries. Jabotinsky, manipulating a machine gun, led the way and soon I was able to flash a message to General Chaytor that the ford was ours. He immediately sent his cavalry dashing across and, after ten days of fierce fighting, the Fourth Turkish Army was destroyed and the battle for Palestine won. Everything we were set to do we did promptly and efficiently and gained the warmest praise from every general we served under, including such noted men as Field Marshal Lord Allenby and General Sir Edward Chaytor. Indeed, the latter, in a special parade of the Legion, told the men that by "their gallantry east of the Jordan they had materially helped toward the winning of the great victory gained at Damascus."

These Legionaries were predominantly British Jews. There were some six thousand others who came from the United States and Canada, principally from the former. Most of the Americans who participated in battle filled the ranks of the 39th Battalion of the Royal Fusiliers, under Colonel Margolin. They showed what mettle they were made of when they took part in the final assault and helped drive the Turks headlong over Moab and out of Palestine.

In December, 1918, while stationed at Rafah on the Egyptian-Palestine border, we were joined by some two thousand Jews from the United States, a fine body of husky men. They arrived in the nick of time and became the mainstay of the British authorities in Palestine when mutiny broke out in Egypt and most of the regular troops had to be dispatched there to suppress the uprising.

The American soldiers proved themselves capable of coping with every difficulty and trial that presented itself, and carried out their arduous duties most admirably. The great majority of them returned to the United States on demobilization and, strange to state, I met quite a number of my old Legionaries at a luncheon given by them in my honor in New York in April, 1945.

The function took place at the Commodore Hotel, the leading

figure in the happy reunion being my old "comrade-in-arms," Elias Ginsburg. We did not forget to toast "absent friends," and stood reverently in silent memory of that greatest of all Legionaries, Vladimir Jabotinsky. We were privileged to have with us the devoted and charming wife of our departed leader, Mme. Jeanne Jabotinsky.

IV

On the morrow of that memorable day in September, 1939, when Neville Chamberlain declared that a state of war existed between Great Britain and Germany, I received a telephone call from Jabotinsky asking me whether I could come to London to discuss a matter of importance. I came to London the same afternoon.

Even before Jabotinsky had time to tell what the important matter was, I knew what he had in mind. Two people cannot be bound spiritually and politically, as Jabotinsky and I were, without acquiring the same way of thinking. It was obvious to me that Jabotinsky would suggest a plan for Jewish national participation in the war.

This time it was not a Jewish Legion that Jabotinsky had in mind, but a Jewish Army with all the paraphernalia of a full-fledged Allied nation. The position which we faced in 1939 was entirely different from that of 1914. In the First World War there was a theoretic possibility for the Jews to ally themselves with either of the warring alliances. It is true that Jewish sympathies traditionally favored Great Britain, but Czarist Russia was Britain's ally at that time. Helping Britain meant also helping the land famous for its pogroms and anti-Jewish persecutions. Now, the Jewish people had no choice whatsoever. Whoever would fight the Nazi-Fascist axis could be assured of the wholehearted support of the Jewish people.

Nor was the object of organized Jewish participation in the war the same as in World War I. Then, the liberation of Palestine from Turkey's rule was the only aim. When the Jewish Legion was formed, it had been stipulated that it could be used only on the Palestinian front and nowhere else. Now, it was not Palestine that had to be liberated, but the world at large was to be cleansed of the Nazi plague. No one on this earth could feel more acutely the barbarity and absurdity of Nazism than the Jew did. Jabotinsky's plan of a Jewish Army had no strings attached to it. He offered to Britain an army 250,000 to 500,000 strong, which would fight under the Supreme Allied Command on *any* front. Nor did he ask for political compensations or guarantees. In his heart he knew, of course, that if a sizable Jewish Army took an active part in the war, the Jewish people would get its political compensation after the war. Palestine would be Jewish, whether an official pledge to this effect was given or not. But he demanded no promises or pledges whatsoever. He just offered an army.

Together we went knocking on the doors of the mighty, from the prime minister down. In one ministry after another we had speech with high officials. Jabotinsky was very eloquent in outlining the great asset which a Jewish Army would prove to the Allied cause. He also offered to organize a worldwide Jewish Intelligence Service, explaining that the Jews, by virtue of their dispersion and the important part they play in international trade, could render outstanding services, particularly in the economic warfare against the enemy and in preventing any leaks in the blockade of Germany.

Some of the British officials were greatly impressed by Jabotinsky's plan. Indeed, it was difficult for anyone not to discern the important potentialities of a Jewish Army and of a Jewish Intelligence Service, especially in a war against Nazism. No one could doubt the unanimity and wholeheartedness of the Jewish hatred for Germany and the determination with which the Jews would fight the Nazi beast. However, neither clear thinking nor justice prevailed in the councils of the British Government and the plan for organized Jewish participation in the war was cold-shouldered and blocked.

The pretexts given by British statesmen for their rejection of the Jewish Army plan changed from time to time. First – in the days of Neville Chamberlain – the official explanation was that Britain and France needed no manpower. They did not know what to do with their own "great armies." This sounds quaint, but nevertheless such was the official answer given to us by the British Government. It was the time of the "phony war" between the Maginot and the Siegfried Lines; and Chamberlain, famous for his lack of vision, might indeed have believed that the small British Army would, with the French, sit forever behind the Maginot fortifications.

Later, after Churchill took over, a new pretext was provided. Both Jabotinsky and myself were at that time already in America. The "phony" stage of the war was long gone. Indeed, the *Wehrmacht* was omnipotent in Europe and the main battlefield had shifted toward the Near East. To say that Britain had enough soldiers was impossible. In fact, Britain badly needed additional manpower. A Jewish Army, however, was still not wanted, so another dishonest rejection scheme was invented. We were told that because of a shortage in arms and ammunition Britain could not agree to the formation of a Jewish Army....

All through the years of the war, even after Jabotinsky passed away, public opinion both in the United States and in Britain clamored for a Jewish Army. The seed sown by Jabotinsky, who came to this country for this very purpose, had borne fruit. But the anti-Zionism of the British Colonial Office proved stronger than the vital interests of Britain and America. Having to make a choice between the acceptance of an army which would undoubtedly make a great contribution to the winning of the war (especially on the Middle Eastern front), or the granting of recognition to the Jewish people, Britain chose to disregard the best interests of the war effort and squashed the army. The strong public demands were of no avail. Whitehall anti-Jewish bureaucrats had decreed that there would be no Jewish Army, and there was no Jewish Army. The Jewish Brigade, formed late in the war, was a most reluctant concession to the widespread demands of public opinion. It was the only tangible achievement of the Jabotinsky idea of a Jewish Army.

Even this Vladimir Jabotinsky did not live to see. He died a heartbroken man at a time when the entire world situation was at its blackest, and when the Jewish-Zionist situation oozed desolation. Yet, in summing up Jabotinsky's life, especially that phase which was devoted to the Jewish Legion in World War I, and his efforts on behalf of a Jewish Army in World War II, one must admit that he accomplished results of historic significance. The two revolutions which he set out to perform nigh thirty years ago were successfully concluded. It was Jabotinsky's Jewish Legion that gave all the actuality and plausibility to the Jewish Army idea in this war. To make the British Government accede to the formation of a Jewish Army was beyond Jabotinsky's power. It was he, however, his ideology, his life, his education, the example of his Legion, that made Jews and Zionists of all parties unite in the demand for Jewish national participation in this war. It was Jabotinsky's spirit that moved thousands of American and British leaders in politics, literature, religion, journalism and arts to raise their voices in favor of a Jewish Army.

I can think of no more fitting conclusion to this effort at evaluation of Vladimir Jabotinsky than a story told years ago by a friend of mine and a close collaborator of Jabotinsky's. Late in 1937, on a visit to Palestine, he met an Englishman who was the head of a great British enterprise in Palestine, who had lived there for many years and was well conversant with Jewish-Zionist politics. When in the course of the conversation the Englishman learned that my friend was an associate of Jabotinsky's, he said: "Oh, you are a follower of Jabotinsky. That's your Churchill."

I never forgot this story, for the parallel between Jabotinsky and Churchill was truly striking. At that time, in 1937, Churchill was still in opposition. He was the *enfant terrible* of British politics for many decades, exactly like Jabotinsky in Zionism. Both Vladimir Jabotinsky and Winston Churchill were great writers and famous orators; both were "civilians" whose lives were colored by military episodes and a deep interest in war problems; both spent the major part of their lives in opposition; both had the foresight and the prophetic power to foretell political events and they both repeatedly warned their peoples – in vain – against the fatal policies of their mediocre leaders.

This parallel is true even in details. When, at a Zionist Congress, the word would spread that Jabotinsky was going to speak, there would be a stampede for seats. They would all listen, applaud and admire, and then they would vote for Weizmann and re-elect him to the leadership. The reaction to Churchill's speeches in the House of Commons was exactly the same. There, too, a half-empty room would fill to capacity to listen to Winnie; they would give him a great cheer, and they would walk into the division lobby to uphold Stanley Baldwin, Ramsay MacDonald, Neville Chamberlain, or some other nonentity.

Unfortunately, this parallel did not proceed to the very end. The British nation, when confronted with a great catastrophe, obeyed its inherent healthy instinct and called to power its Jabotinsky, who was destined to lead Britain out of its dire peril to glorious victory.

The Jewish people did not turn to its Churchill. Even facing the most tragic disaster in its long and eventful history, it still left the reins in the hands of its old leaders. The Jewish Churchill was left to die "in opposition."

But I am convinced that Vladimir Jabotinsky did not die a defeated man. On the contrary, before he passed away he had vitalized and given hope to the youth of Israel, and this seed, which he sowed in adversity, will, before a generation passes, assuredly flower into victory.

La Jolla, June 28, 1945.

The Story of the Jewish Legion

Chapter 1
Birth of the Legion Idea

Early in December, 1914, I arrived in Alexandria from Civitavecchia on an Italian ship. The British customs official was fumbling with my Russian passport, trying to ferret out from the jumble of thirty odd visas my permit to land in Egypt; at the same time he was chatting with some officers among our fellow passengers, and suddenly I heard him say, "A few days ago a boatful of Zionists, almost a thousand of them, arrived from Jaffa – the Turks kicked them out of Palestine."

The war was in its fifth month, and for more than three months I had been wandering over the cheerless world as a correspondent of *Russkiya Vyedomosti* (Russian Monitor). My mission was to report on the moods and sentiments produced by the war rather than on the war itself. In Sweden I had to establish whether the public shared Sven Hedin's belief that Russia, barred as she was from Constantinople and the warm Bosphorus, intended to seize a Norwegian port – Narvik, or perhaps Bergen – and thus acquire an unfreezing harbor on the warm Gulf Stream; and if so, whether Sweden would join Germany and declare war on Russia. My task in England was to determine what truth, if any, there was in the biting quip then popular in Russia that "the British Lion is prepared to fight to the last drop of Russian blood." In France there was nothing to "investigate" – not even skeptics had any doubts about the feelings of the French. I was simply to report on the conditions at the front, if I could get there; go to Rheims to see whether the Germans had really shot to pieces its magnificent cathedral; find out whether Paris was "dispirited" or "optimistic." But by the time I reached France, "Paris" had already been transferred to Bordeaux, as the government offices had been forced temporarily to move out of the threatened capital. I went to Bordeaux – and there, one wet morning, I read in a poster pasted on a wall that Turkey had joined the Central Powers and begun military operations.

I must confess: until that morning, in Bordeaux as everywhere else, I had been a mere observer, without any particular reasons for wishing full triumph to one side and crushing disaster to the other. My desire at that time was: stalemate, and peace as soon as possible. Turkey's move transformed me in one short morning into a fanatical believer in war until victory; Turkey's move made this war "my war." In 1909 I had been chief editor in Constantinople of four Zionist newspapers at the same time (the sort of thing that occurs only in one's youth); the Young Turks then ruled the Sublime Porte, and there and then I reached the steadfast conviction that where the Turk rules neither sun may shine nor grass may grow, and that the only hope for the restoration of Palestine lay in the dismemberment of the Ottoman Empire. That morning in Bordeaux, after reading the damp poster on the wall, I drew the only logical conclusion possible – and to this day I don't understand why it took numbers of my friends so many years to reach such a simple conclusion. As I saw it, the matter was crystal clear: the fate of the Jews in Russia, Poland, Galicia – very important undoubtedly – was, if viewed in the historical perspective only, something temporary as compared to the revolution in Jewish national life which the dismemberment of Turkey would bring us.

I never doubted that once Turkey entered the war, she would be defeated and sliced to pieces: here again I am at a loss to understand how anyone could ever have had any doubts on this subject. It was no guesswork but a matter of cold statistical calculation. I am glad of the opportunity to mention it here, as I have been accused of gambling on a problematic winner in those years. I had lived in Turkey for a long time as a newspaper correspondent. I have the highest regard for the profession of journalist: a conscientious correspondent knows much more about the country he writes from than any ambassador – in my experience, often more than most of the local professors. But in that particular instance not only professors but even ambassadors were aware of the pretty obvious truth about Turkey. That Germany would be beaten into unconditional surrender, of course, not even a journalist could have foreseen at that time. But that Turkey more than anyone else would have to pay for this war, I did not and could not doubt for one moment. Stone and iron can endure a fire; a wooden hut must burn, and no miracle will save it.

Exactly at what moment I conceived the idea of a Jewish fighting force – whether there in Bordeaux in front of that poster, or later – I don't remember now. I think, however, there never was any such moment. Where is the man, whatever his faith, who can honestly point his finger at a certain date and say, "This is where I saw the light"? Everyone is born with the germ of his belief somewhere inside his brain, though it may not manifest itself until old age, however. I believe that it was always clear to me – from birth so to speak – that if ever a war should occur between England and Turkey, the right thing for the Jews would be to form a regiment of their own and participate in the conquest of Palestine – although before that day in Bordeaux I had never thought about it distinctly. As a matter of fact, this idea is a very normal idea which would have occurred, under such circumstances, to any normal person; and I claim the title of a fully normal person. In Jewish colloquial parlance this title is sometimes expressed as a *Goyishe kop*; if it is true – so much the worse for us.

A few days later I cabled to my paper in Moscow: "Suggest tour Moslem countries of North Africa to study effect on local population of Holy War proclaimed by Sultan." My editor cabled back: "Go ahead."

I began with Morocco but purposely went there via Madrid, where Max Nordau lived at that time; at the very outset of the war somebody in Paris conceived the bright idea of banishing him from France, his true homeland, as a "Hungarian." Terrible things were happening then in the world....

I asked Nordau, "If the English could be persuaded to form a Jewish unit to fight on the Eastern front – in Palestine – what would be your attitude?"

He was skeptical. A sound idea, but where could such a unit get soldiers? English, French, Russian Jews were serving in their respective armies; in the neutral countries in Europe there were few Jews; America was far away; and besides, Jews nourished some foolish sentimental predilection for the Turk, "our cousin Ishmael." True, no scholar on earth could tell what relation the Turks, a Touranian tribe, could possibly be to Ishmael the Semite, but there it was, and Nordau himself had had to face that music after his famous rebuke to the Young Turks at the Hamburg Congress.

"I remember that speech of yours," said I. "You declared: 'Why go to Turkey, to get assimilated there? That we can have nearer and cheaper.' I then came to Hamburg from Constantinople and cheered wildly."

"And I," he replied, "had no end of trouble with some of our sentimental idiots. How dared I speak so harshly about our 'cousin'?"

"Doctor," I said, "we cannot let idiots dictate our policy. Not only are the Turks no cousins of ours; even with the real Ishmael we have nothing in common. We belong to Europe, thank God: for two thousand years we helped to build European civilization. And here comes one more quotation from another of your speeches: 'We are going to Palestine to extend the moral boundaries of Europe as far as the Euphrates.' Our worst enemy in this undertaking is the Turk. Now that the hour of his downfall has struck, we cannot possibly stand by and do nothing, can we?"

The old sage replied to my question with a profound saying; it wasn't until much later that I came to realize how profound it was.

He shook his wise head and said, "This, my young friend, is logic; but logic is a Greek art, and Jews can't stand it. The Jew learns not by way of reason but from catastrophes. He won't buy an umbrella merely because he sees clouds in the sky; he waits until he is drenched and catches pneumonia – then he makes up his mind."

Much time elapsed before I appreciated the whole truth of this remark; by that time I had found out that there existed in the world yet another tribe with exactly the same attitude toward logic, clouds and umbrellas – the English. The difference is that their lungs are stronger, and they have more money to pay the doctor.

After that conversation I visited Morocco, Algiers and Tunis, trying to "investigate" whether there had been any response to the Turkish appeal and whether there was any real danger of a Moslem rising. To ask the Moslems themselves for information would have been utterly useless, of course. Those people are great diplomats (in that "classical" sense to which I shall have to revert when I come to my audience with Delcassé), especially when they are afraid. I chose a better way: I questioned the local Sephardic merchants. They are not less autochthonous, and they are more clever and more frank. Where his own Jewish interests are not concerned, the Jew's vision is likely to be perfectly sharp and farsighted. He knows the true feelings of the Arabs: even when they tell him stories, he can interpret their deceptions and draw his conclusions from what they don't tell him. Almost all those Sephardim – merchants, lawyers, journalists, from Tangiers to Tunis – gave me the same answer, and history proved they were right.

"The appeal to a Holy War? Nonsense. Ridiculous even to ask. Only you naive Europeans still believe that it is possible to raise masses in the Orient in the name of Islamic solidarity and make them accept any serious risks. The Turks themselves don't believe it: for the last hundred years Europe has been inflicting on them defeat after defeat, stripping them of their best provinces one after another, yet not one single Moslem people has budged an inch during all this time to help the Sultan – even though they call him 'Caliph of all the Moslems.'

The Germans, who are just as naive as all other Europeans, have persuaded the Turks to try once more. It is hopeless: not a soul here will lift a finger to help the Turks."

From Tunis I went to Egypt, via Rome. In Alexandria I unexpectedly found a lively Zionist atmosphere. Over a thousand refugees were there from Jaffa. Suddenly, for no reason at all, the Turks had ordered the Arab police to catch Jews in the streets and to pack them into boats. The police – "Cousin Ishmael" – carried out these orders with great enthusiasm, not sparing blows and not stopping short of loot. And on the water, a hundred meters from the Italian steamer, the Arab owner would stop his boat and demand a pound from each "passenger," threatening to throw them into the sea if they did not pay.

I tried very hard to understand why the Jews, and nobody else, were chosen for expulsion. Among the refugees there were merchants, workmen, students, doctors, women and children. To this day I do not know what the underlying idea was....

In Egypt the British Government provided barracks and money. A special department was created for the affairs of the refugees, with a fine, friendly Englishman, Mr. Hornblower, in charge. The name of the woman who took care of the largest of the barracks – Gabbari – was Broadbent. The children used to call her the "white lady."

I worked in Gabbari for several weeks. It was a camp of twelve hundred souls, of whom three hundred were Sephardim. We had two kitchens, an Ashkenazic and a Sephardic (at first there had been only one, but the Sephardim rebelled because they could not tolerate Ashkenazic food, especially the soup). We also had a Hebrew school and a chemist, and were altogether a completely independent community, having even a regiment of watchmen. There were about twelve languages besides Hebrew spoken in the camp. It was fortunate that all the children, nearly all the men and some of the women knew Hebrew. Otherwise, I cannot imagine how such a community could have been organized – with Bukharans, Moroccans, Grusinians (Georgians), Spaniards, and Jaffa students who refused to take quinine unless the chemist spoke Hebrew. I remember that a few weeks later these students organized a football club and won a match against the scouts of Alexandria.

Every morning a huge army wagon used to arrive, driven by an Australian soldier and led by two gigantic Australian horses, for the express purpose of giving the smaller children of the camp a "ride." The Australians learned to call out in Hebrew, "Come on, children," and in a moment the wagon would be filled with tiny mites.

Occasionally we received a visit from one of the Australian officers, Lieutenant Eliezer Margolin, who stood and watched, and babbled in broken Yiddish, never for a moment dreaming that in a few years he would be colonel of one of the Jewish Battalions and that these very watchmen would be among his men.

The Sephardic community of Alexandria magnanimously opened its heart and its purse. The Chief Rabbi, Raphael della Pergola (he has since died), his assistant, Haham Abraham Abichezer, Edgar Suares the banker, and the merchant Joseph de Picciotto, all worked in the office, collected money, clothes, bedclothes, and represented the refugees at the government offices. There was also no lack of workers from the Ashkenazic side. Old Z. D. Levontin, manager of our bank in Palestine, procured credit from the Egyptian Bank and distributed money among those refugees who had deposits in Jaffa. V. Z. Gluskin, president of the Rishon-le-Zion winegrowers, used to ride around on tours of inspection from one barracks to another. M. Margolis, a leading representative of Nobel's Oil Company in the Orient, was the treasurer.

There were also non-Jewish voluntary helpers. Especially do I remember the beautiful Frenchwoman, the wife of the Jewish Baron Felix de Menasseh: whenever she brought a wagon-load of fresh bread to Gabbari I used to wonder at the clever manner in which she was dressed. Very simply, and yet with "chic." It seemed as if the French modistes had a special model – styles for visiting the poor.

Here in Gabbari the Jewish Legion was born. Two people played an important part in its birth – the Russian consul, Petrov, and Joseph Trumpeldor.

Chapter 11

First Experiment – Zion Mule Corps

Consul Petrov was a fervent Russian patriot. Whether he hated Jews I do not know; I cannot understand why we should always have to examine this corner of the souls of Gentiles. But he certainly was a patriot and a stiff, wooden bureaucrat of the old classic school. Among the young people in our camp there were several hundred Russian Jews. In terms of the "capitulations" treaty entered into between Russia and Egypt, Petrov had extraterritorial jurisdiction over all Russian subjects in Egypt; now he suddenly demanded that these young men should return to Russia and join the army.

The position was an unpleasant one. Under the terms of the treaty, the British Administration in Egypt was fully expected to accede to such a demand and was even obliged to employ every means at its disposal to carry it out.

A deputation waited on the English governor (he was styled, "adviser to the governor," but of course it was he who was the real boss). And at that interview I, an old admirer of Sephardi Jews (they are the finest Jews in the world), discovered another quality, which I had not known them to possess – the courage with which a Sephardi addresses the governor of a country at war.

The spokesman of the delegation was Edgar Suares, a rich banker, a man of over fifty and a diehard assimilationist. I suppose he was the governor's frequent opponent at poker in the club. Still, a governor is a governor.

"Do you remember, Your Excellency," asked Suares, "what happened here in Alexandria two years ago, when Consul Petrov wanted to arrest that Russian Jew, R—, who had been a 'political' offender in Russia?"

"I remember," said the governor, a trifle troubled, for he had not forgotten the gigantic demonstration of ten thousand Sephardim in the streets, and he knew that Suares himself had been at the head of that demonstration.

"Do you remember," asked Suares again, "how you had to call out the firemen to drive away the demonstrators by turning the hoses on them – and still the Jew, R—, was not given up?"

"Of course I remember!" answered the governor with a smile, for after all he was a sportsman and loved a prank. "What could I do when some rascal cut the hose?"

"I was that rascal!" replied Suares proudly.

The governor burst out laughing.

"Hush," he said. "Your young fellows will not be given away either.... Still, the position is complicated...a treaty...time of war, but there's no question of giving up your men...."

After this visit I went to make the acquaintance of Trumpeldor. I knew that he was among the refugees, but I had not yet seen him. He lived somewhere in a private house. Consul Petrov, whatever else he may have been, was a man of principle. As soon as he learned that there was among the refugees a Russian ex-officer who had lost his left arm at Port Arthur, he sent his secretary to inform him that he could obtain from the consulate the monthly pension to which he was entitled. Trumpeldor, therefore, did not require any help. On the contrary – he even rendered assistance to others.

I had heard of Trumpeldor while I was still in Russia.

He was born in the Caucasus in the year 1880. His father was one of those men of iron endurance who went through the hell of Nicholas I's barracks – twenty-five years' service – losing neither their health nor their Jewishness. Joseph was not admitted into the university on account of the *numerus clausus*; so he became a dentist. Then came military service and the Russo-Japanese War. Trumpeldor's regiment was sent to Port Arthur, and there he lived through eleven terrible months of siege. There he lost his left arm, almost to the shoulder. But no sooner had he come out of hospital than he demanded to be sent back to the front. After the fall of Port Arthur he was taken prisoner by the Japanese, together with the rest of General Stoessel's Army. In captivity he organized Zionist societies and collected money for the Jewish National Fund.

After the war he was granted a reserve officer's rank, and until 1917 he was, as far as I know, the only Jewish officer in the Russian Army. He entered the University of St. Petersburg, completed his law studies and immediately left for Palestine. There he worked in Degania and other Socialist settlements, and all his comrades agree that with his one arm he was yet the strongest and the best of agricultural laborers.

Trumpeldor's friend, the late D. Belotzerkovsky, told me the following story, which occurred during the time when he still had both arms. He held the highest rank then allowed to a Jew, something between a private and a sergeant (this latter dignity being inaccessible to Jews), and his section was entrenched on a hill before a Russian fort. The Japanese pressed them hard: nearly all the adjoining hills had already been evacuated, and in Trumpeldor's section all senior officers had been killed – except a second lieutenant from the reserve, who had gone to ask for orders and had not returned. The soldiers began to grumble and to crawl toward the end of the trench. Trumpeldor placed himself at the outlet, his finger on the trigger of his gun, and said, "I'll shoot the first man who makes a move." So they remained in the trench until the last of the neighboring hills had been evacuated by the Russians. Then Trumpeldor sent his men into the fort, but he himself stayed and crawled out to reconnoiter: he looked the situation over and came to the conclusion that the Japanese could still be driven out. In the plain, away from the firing, he saw an officer wearing the uniform of captain of the marine corps, with binoculars in his hands. Trumpeldor went down to him and explained: "With a fresh company stationed over there, we could yet retake the position."

"Right you are," said the captain. "Run over behind that mound. My men are there; tell the lieutenant to bring them here."

Trumpeldor reached that hill, which was shelled heavily by the Japanese, climbed to the top – and saw that the marines were not there. They had "withdrawn." He went back and reported to the captain, who was deeply grieved: he tore off his cap, struck his gray-haired head with his fist and groaned, "What a shame! Took to their heels – like kikes!"

Trumpeldor afterward confirmed that story to me, smiling very merrily.

I found him at home. He looked very much like an Englishman or a Swede. Rather tall and very slim, with close-cropped hair, he was clean-shaven, with thin lips and a quiet smile. He spoke Russian excellently, though under the influence of Palestine he had developed a slight singsong intonation. His Hebrew was slow, and poor in words – but it sufficed. His Yiddish was atrocious. He was well educated, well read in Russian literature, and apparently gave much thought to every line he read. To this day I do not know whether he was what we Jews call "clever." I rather think not: in this term of ours there is a conglomeration of meanings: acuteness, sharpness, over-sharpness, a knack of twisting the meanings of quite simple words, of pondering deeply over non-essentials, of joking when others are serious – and generally doing the simplest things in an ostentatiously complicated way. These qualities, I found, he fortunately did not possess. But he did have a clear, straight mind and a deep quiet humor which assisted him in distinguishing between the important and the unimportant. And even when he found something to be important, he discussed it without heat, without noise and alarums, not for one moment losing his sense of proportion. His speech was sober and restrained, with no sentimentalism, no pathos – and no "strong language." This latter even the company at the barracks had not taught him. I must admit that when I speak Russian and become excited, I make use of all the unprintable words in the Russian vocabulary. I think I exhibited this sort of fluency in Trumpeldor's presence on two occasions. He was not shocked. He even smiled and said, "*zdorovo*" (well done) in the manner of an impartial literary critic who has just listened to a poem. But I never heard him curse, except perhaps for the word *shelma*, which has the same mild meaning as "rascal" in English. In Hebrew his favorite expression was *en davar* (never mind); and they say it was with these words on his lips that he died, five years later, at Tel Hai. There was a complete philosophy contained in this *en davar*: do not exaggerate; do not see danger where none exists; do not regard a man who does his duty as a hero – for history is long, the Jewish people everlasting, and truth is sacred, but everything else, trouble and care and pain and death, *en davar*.

He was served better by his one arm than many of us are served by two. He washed and shaved and dressed, he ate, polished his boots, drove his horse and shot – all with his single arm. His room was remarkably tidy, his clothes were clean and brushed, his bearing quiet and courteous. For many years he had been a vegetarian, a Socialist and a pacifist – but he was not one of those pacifists who sit tight, letting others fight and die....

We did not talk long that day; one did not have to speak much to him. Not being "clever," he was the quicker at grasping the essence of a subject, and in a quarter of an hour he would give you his reply – "yes" or "no." His reply to me was "yes."

In the evening the members of the committee to help the refugees gathered at the apartment of M. A. Margolis; besides our host there were present Dr. Weitz from Jerusalem, V. Gluskin, G. Horodetsky, an

American tourist G. Caplan, Z. Levontin, Trumpeldor, J. Ettinger the farming expert, and myself. I enumerate the names so carefully because if that gathering had voted against our plan, there would probably have been nothing to write about today. But the vote was favorable: five against two, one member abstaining. The record of that meeting, dated 16th Adar 5675, is preserved by V. Z. Gluskin in Tel Aviv.

A week later we called a meeting of our young people in the Mafruza barracks. About two hundred were present, and on the platform were Chief Rabbi della Pergola, other members of the committee which had charge of the refugees, among them old Mr. Gluskin, and Trumpeldor. We gave the gathering a review of the position. The English would not do what Consul Petrov had demanded, but it was not desirable to remain in the barracks indefinitely. Sooner or later the English forces would leave Egypt for Palestine. From Jaffa bad news was arriving daily. The Turks had forbidden Hebrew shop signs in the streets; they had deported Dr. Ruppin, the representative of the Zionist Actions Committee, even though he was a German citizen; they had arrested the leading members of the Yishuv, and had declared that they would not allow any Jewish colonization to continue after the war. Therefore? …

Some day our national library in Jerusalem will get the document that was signed that spring night in the dim hall of Mafruza. It is a piece of paper torn out of an exercise book, on which is written a resolution in Hebrew, "To form a Jewish Legion and to propose to England to make use of it in Palestine," and it bears about one hundred signatures. The first signature was that of Mr. Ze'ev Gluskin.

"I am old," he said, snatching the pen from my hand. "I am useless as a soldier, but I want to bear the responsibility."

Next day, as I was coming into the Gabbari courtyard, I saw a complete parade. Three groups of young men were learning to march, having chosen their own instructors from among Russian ex-soldiers; several girls were stitching a flag in a corner, and a committee of schoolboys was engaged in translating military terminology into Hebrew. Then Trumpeldor arrived. The three groups formed a column of files and marched past him in a kind of ceremonial procession. He watched with a satisfied smile.

"Good heavens," I whispered to him, "they march like geese."

"*En davar*," he replied.

Several days later a delegation went out to Cairo, the winter seat of the Egyptian Government. The delegation first presented itself to the minister of the interior, Mr. Ronald Graham (styled "adviser to…"). Today he is known as Sir Ronald Graham, and has since been ambassador in Rome. He is a cool, taciturn Scotsman who asks few questions but gets things done with speed and precision. Later, in 1916 and 1917, I met him in London, at the head of the Department for Near Eastern Affairs, and he was, perhaps, the man who did most to assist Dr. Weizmann in obtaining the Balfour Declaration, and me in my fight for the Jewish Legion plan. This time, in Cairo, he listened, nodded his head in agreement, asked, "How many men do you expect?", wrote something in a notebook, and said curtly, "It does not rest with me, but I shall try."

The second visit was to General Maxwell, who commanded the small British Force in Egypt. We were introduced by Cattaoui Pasha, a fine old Sephardi gentleman, one of the most respected men in all Egypt. The other delegates, besides myself, were Trumpeldor, Levontin, Gluskin and Margolis. We forced poor Trumpeldor to put on his four St. George Crosses – two bronze and two golden. The general looked at him sharply and asked abruptly in French, "Port Arthur, I understand?"

But his reply to our proposal was profoundly disappointing.

"I have heard nothing about an offensive in Palestine, and I doubt whether such an offensive will be launched at all. I am prohibited by regulations from admitting foreign soldiers into the British Army. I can make only one suggestion – that your young men form themselves into a detachment for mule transport, to be made use of on some other sector of the Turkish front. I cannot do more than that."

That night, in Mr. Gluskin's hotel apartment, we sat up till dawn debating the situation: what should we do?

We civilians felt that General Maxwell's offer must be politely declined. The term he had used in French, *corps de muletiers,* had a most unflattering sound in our civilian ears: what a shocking combination – Zion, the rebirth of a nation, the first really Jewish troop in the whole history of the Exile, and "mules." Secondly: "Another Turkish front," he had said. What had we to do with "other fronts"? We didn't even know for certain what "other front" he had meant: the first attempt to conquer Gallipoli from the sea had already ended in failure; and as to the probability of an impending second attack, this time with infantry landing on the peninsula – this, as yet, was only a whispered rumor. One thing only was clear: they would not be sent to Palestine. The offer must be rejected.

Trumpeldor disagreed with us.

"Talking as a soldier," he said, "I think you overrate the difference. Trenches or transport is practically the same – all so essential that you can't do without it; and even the danger is often the same. You are just afraid of the word 'mules,' and that is childish."

"But a mule," somebody interrupted, "is almost a donkey. Sounds like calling names, especially in Yiddish."

"In Yiddish," Trumpeldor retorted, "'horse' is also not a compliment: '*sei nit kein ferd.*'.... Yet if it were to be a cavalry detachment you would all feel terribly proud. In French, to call a person *chameau* is grossly offensive, but they have a Camel Corps in the French Army, and in the English Army, too; and to serve in them is considered a particular honor. It's all nonsense."

"But that 'other front' which is not Palestine..."

"Also not at all essential, speaking as a soldier. To get the Turk out of Palestine we've got to smash the Turk. Which side you begin the smashing, north or south, is just technique. Any front leads to Zion."

Nothing was decided that night. Alone with Trumpeldor on the way back to our hotel, I said to him, "You may be right; but I, personally, would not join a unit of that sort."

"I probably will," he said.

Next morning, back in Alexandria, I found a cablegram on my table from Genoa. It was signed, "Rutenberg": he wanted to know whether we could meet "at once" and where. Of course I knew who he was and what he stood for. I had never met him, but in Rome, just before I sailed for Egypt, the Russian journalist, Amphiteatroff, had mentioned him to me.

"Just fancy who has suddenly become an ardent Zionist! Peter Rutenberg. He says that Turkey's entry into the war has opened up splendid vistas for the Jews, and I suspect he is ruminating on all kinds of great schemes. By the way, he knows a number of influential politicians, both here and in France."

Having read the cable, I immediately went to find Trumpeldor and said: "Joseph Vladimirovitch, I'm off to Europe. Should General Maxwell change his mind and agree to form a real fighting regiment, send me a cable and I'll come back at once; if not, I'll try to find some other generals."

Toward the middle of April, 1915, at Brindisi, I met Rutenberg; and there was a cable waiting for me at the Post Office, signed "Trumpeldor." It read, "Maxwell's offer accepted."

I am not writing history; I am writing my personal recollections. I never saw the Gallipoli Campaign, and it is therefore not for me to tell the story of Trumpeldor's unit, the "Zion Mule Corps." But one thing I admit: I had been wrong; Trumpeldor was right. Those six hundred muleteers actually opened up a new avenue in the development of Zionist possibilities. Until then it had been almost impossible to talk Zionism even to friendly statesmen: at such a cruel time as that, who could really expect them to worry about agricultural settlements or the renaissance of Hebrew? All that was, for the moment, simply outside their field of vision. It was the little transport unit in Gallipoli which succeeded in breaking through that hedge, in putting at least a name, a hint, a question mark on the map of that inaccessible, walled-in horizon of a world busy with war. All the European papers mentioned the Jewish unit; nearly all the military correspondents allowed on the Gallipoli Peninsula devoted a passage in their reports to it; later, a page in their books. In short, all through the first half of the war that mule corps proved to be the only manifestation that somehow reminded the "world," especially Great Britain's military "world," that Zionism could also be "topical," a part of "actuality," and perhaps capable of being transformed into a factor that might prove of some value even under gunfire. For me, personally, throughout the whole struggle I was destined to experience in working for the realization of the Legion plan, the Zion Mule Corps was a sort of open sesame which gained me admission to the War Office in London, to M. Delcassé's sanctum at the Quai d'Orsay in Paris, and to the Ministry of Foreign Affairs in St. Petersburg.

But even as a purely military experience, the story of our Gallipoli unit makes a fine chapter in our Jewish military annals. I regret that Trumpeldor's Palestinian friends have proved to be too hasty in publishing his private letters from Gallipoli. He had written them to a dearly beloved friend, in great intimacy, enumerating all the drawbacks and worries of a campaign's humdrum everyday life, with that interest in detail which was one of his advantages as a captain of men. Camp life, under Gallipoli conditions, could often not help appearing sordid. Look at any of the great Garibaldi's romantic campaigns: half of their inside life, too, often consisted of kitchen trouble, quarrels between Ensign A and Lieutenant B, myriads of tiny disappointments. What has all this to do with the real meaning of a collective sacrifice? From the first day of Churchill's ill-omened venture till its very last night, this bunch of young refugees honestly carried on their hard and risky service under enemy fire. In this, too, Trumpeldor proved right: trenches or transport – they all had to face the same danger. The whole area occupied by British troops was just a few square miles, every bit of it well within the range of the Turkish guns on the hilltop of Achi-Baba, which peppered equally both front trench and mule camp. Every night under that bombardment they had to lead their loaded mules to the front and back. Their losses in dead and wounded were hardly different, in proportion, from those of any other section of Gallipoli: some of them now wear medals; all of them did their bit with courage and dignity. It was especially their courage that struck General Ian Hamilton, G.O.C., of the Gallipoli Expeditionary Force, who wrote to me after the close of that campaign, on November 17, 1915: "The men have done extremely well, working their mules calmly under heavy shell and rifle-fire, and thus showing a more difficult type of bravery than the men in the front line who had the excitement of combat to keep them going."

The Commanding Officer was Lieutenant Colonel John Henry Patterson, one of the most remarkable Christian figures our people ever encountered on its way through all the centuries of the Dispersion. I made his acquaintance much later, so I shall deal with him in the chapters to come. Trumpeldor, to whom the military authorities granted a sort of hemi-demi-semi-honorary captaincy, was second in command for a time, but toward the end of the campaign Patterson fell ill or was wounded – I forget which – and was sent to England for convalescence, leaving Trumpeldor as O.C. Zion Mule Corps. Then the campaign had to be liquidated; for several months, in Alexandria, Trumpeldor struggled against fate in trying to delay the inevitable disbandment of his corps, bombarding Headquarters with collective petitions to allow them to keep together and train "for the impending Palestine offensive." But it was all to no avail. Formed in April, 1915, the Zion Mule Corps was disbanded on May 26, 1916. Not more than about 120 of its soldiers managed subsequently to re-enlist and find their way to London; and this was the nucleus around which the "real" Jewish Legion was ultimately formed; that Legion which, armed with bayonets and Lewis guns, eventually took part in the conquest of Palestine, and some of whose dead now fill the "Shield of David" patch in the War Cemetery on the Mount of Olives in Jerusalem. Trumpeldor was right: though it was in the Jordan Valley that we were victorious, the way through Gallipoli was the right way.

Chapter III
Failure After Failure

There is a strong temptation to tell the story of those summer months of 1915 as briefly as possible – a sad tale of disappointments and failures. Even now I do not relish the memories of that period, though I must admit it taught me a great deal. First of all, I learned the important truth that in a public matter, especially in the struggle for an idea, an initiated project develops essentially through failures. One way or another, every setback proves later to have been a step toward victory. Each defeat brings another host of followers, indeed, right from the ranks of the foes of yesterday. Somehow, all at once, these enemies are struck by the revelation that though they fought against you, deep within their souls they hoped you would win – and your defeat leaves in their hearts an emptiness and a sense of regret....

Those months schooled me in patience: now I could propound a complete theory of patience in several ponderous volumes. The gist of it would be that after every failure it is necessary to examine yourself and ask, "Look here, perhaps you are wrong?" If you are wrong, get off the rostrum and shut up. But if you are right, do not believe your eyes: that defeat is not a defeat. "No," is no answer. Wait an hour and start right over again from the beginning.

That I was right – those months showed me that also beyond any doubt. And at every step I took, and even in everything that my Zionist opponents tried to do, I saw further proof of this truth that, except through the idea of the Legion, it would be impossible to push Zionism into the rank of those questions in which the world might be interested at that extraordinary time. Often, then, I used to recall an anecdote which Nahum Sokolov had told me long before the War.

In 1901, after the Fourth Congress in London, he went for a rest to a health resort in Switzerland. There he became acquainted with a Scotch lord and in the course of their conversation mentioned to him that he had been at the Zionist Congress.

"Oh, yes," said milord. "Zionism, very interesting. If I am not mistaken, my younger brother also belongs to this movement or, at any rate, to something very close to it."

Sokolov was astounded. The nobleman was a devout Catholic; seemingly, his brother also. What did this mean? He began tactfully to ask questions, and soon it became clear that milord's brother was – a vegetarian. Zionism, vegetarianism – for outsiders in the year 1901, it was "the same" movement, or "something very close to it."

So it remained for most European statesmen in the year 1914–15. In Italy, in France, often even in England, one received the same impression: Zionism, as such, did not exist for them at that time. In order to make them see it through the military monocle, it was necessary to put a "practical" point to it – in other words, a bayonet.

I found Rutenberg in Brindisi in a little hotel near the harbor. We met for the first time. He is a tall, broad-shouldered, heavyset man; in every movement, in every word, is the impression of a strong and stern will. I suspect that he knows it and does not like to forget it, and diligently takes care that others, too, shall not forget it for a minute. Who knows – perhaps that's the way to do it? Indeed, a public figure is always on a stage and it is a question whether he ought to appear without makeup. Naturally, I speak not of a false makeup but of one which really fits the essential nature of the actor on the political stage. But no makeup whatsoever could hide the fact that this man had kind eyes and a truly childlike smile. I understand why his subordinates and workers in Palestine obey Rutenberg like an autocrat and love him like a father.

A ten-minute talk was enough to agree on the main subject. Though we had never corresponded, we recognized immediately that we had been thinking of the same thing. And furthermore, though there had been no mention in the press of a single word concerning the Legion in general or of the Alexandrian volunteers, he nevertheless felt sure that I was working toward this end; and I, although A. V. Amphiteatroff had been unable to disclose to me in Rome what Rutenberg's plans were, also understood immediately from his brief telegram why he needed this conference with me. Remarkable. What is the source of that wireless communication between people who, if they met in the street, would not have recognized one another?

In Brindisi Rutenberg and I arrived at three conclusions.

Our first conclusion: to create a Jewish unit – a thing easily done. Human material was available in England, in France; in the neutral countries there were hundreds and thousands of Jewish youth, most of them of Russian origin, who were still in civilian clothes; and though America was far away, still there was America, also.

Second conclusion: the best partner for our venture was certainly England. In that respect our Alexandrian volunteers had acted correctly. But "best" did not mean "sole." Italy was in a turmoil, all agog to fight, and soon would be in the thick of it. Even then, Italy, at a time when no one conceived of a Mussolini, had succeeded in developing a large and healthy appetite for all the shores of the Mediterranean Sea. Even more important, there was France. For five centuries or more France had dreamed of Palestine and Syria as her possessions.

Therefore, it was necessary to try everywhere – in London, in Paris, in Rome.

Third conclusion: in Rome we were to work together. Then, I should go on to Paris and to London and Rutenberg to America.

Our efforts in Italy ended in failure. Despite much public agitation, when it came to a "showdown," neither the cabinet members nor the deputies to whom Rutenberg introduced me or whom I was able to meet through the friends I had made in my student days in Rome – none of them knew whether Italy would get into the war. Both Signor Mosca, Assistant Colonial Secretary, and the late L. Bissolati, leader of the Socialists but a great proponent of the war, told us the same thing.

"If Italy gets into it, then your idea will be just perfect; then, come and see us again and we'll discuss this matter in detail. But now..."

Paris. Again failure.

There I found a warm friend of Zionism in the person of Gustave Hervé. The older generation of readers will still remember his biography. Until the war he was a dyed-in-the-wool pacifist, taking in the course of his life a good deal of punishment for this unpatriotic attitude. To scare the bourgeois he called his Paris paper, *La Guerre Sociale*. But the moment the Germans stepped over the frontiers of Belgium, he changed the name of his journal to *Victoire* and became one of the pillars of warring France. In my opinion he was probably the most gifted journalist among the radicals of France. The government, naturally, treated him with special consideration, according to the ancient truism expressed in the parable of the prodigal son.

Hervé was one of the few people who immediately appreciated the importance of Zionism both in itself and, particularly, for the Empire, which could thus establish a claim on Palestine. He introduced me to the minister of foreign affairs; at that time it was Delcassé. Delcassé is now dead and I do not want to say anything disrespectful about him, but still I shall set down frankly my impression of the man. Our conversation disclosed to me for the first time a secret which later observations amply confirmed: among those fortunate nations which have their states, it is not at all necessary to be a genius to reach first rank among the important statesmen. With us, in the Zionist movement, it takes considerably more....

Aside from that, Delcassé belonged to the old "classic" school of diplomacy which loved to play at "secrets" and whose idea of clever statesmanship was expressed in the famous epigram of Talleyrand: "Speech is the best medium for hiding thought." Possibly this was very clever a hundred years ago, but in our time this infantile cunning has, if I am not mistaken, definitely gone out of style in serious diplomatic circles. However, dear France still goes to the theater to see Racine and believes in all sorts of classicism.

I have not the slightest intention of overestimating my own extremely small role in world events, but I say with profound conviction that during that morning Delcassé lost a great deal at the expense of France: not merely a Jewish Legion but much more. I went to him not only on my own initiative: my visit was partly the result of a conference with Chaim Weizmann. He had been in Paris a few days earlier. At that time he had begun his negotiations with English statesmen and was already convinced of their sympathetic attitude, though he complained that they all still refused to consider Palestine "realistically." But the main obstacle in his path was that the English were afraid to disturb or shock France by making any independent moves which would affect the future of the Holy Land. At that time there was still a sort of international tradition which recognized some nebulous claim that France had to Syria and Palestine. For Zionist diplomacy it was important to know whether the French Government had any definite policy regarding our demands and, especially, whether we could hope for a sympathetic policy. If yes, then it would be necessary to work on two fronts; if no, it would be possible to concentrate all our energy in England to create a favorable attitude toward Zionism, and possibly – what was even more important – to arouse in England an appetite for and an active interest in the idea of a "British Palestine," thereby promoting operations on the Palestine front.

For many reasons Weizmann found it inconvenient to put this question to the French Government himself. He returned to London and there awaited the results of my meeting with Delcassé.

I phrased the question in this form: "If at the end of the War, Palestine were to fall into the French sphere of influence, may we Zionists trust that the French Government will take into consideration our national aspirations?"

He replied immediately in that irritable tone with which one answers a question that has already caused one a great deal of annoyance. "I do not believe it possible that Palestine will go to any one of the great Powers; no, the others will not consent to that."

"Understood," I said, "but in that event there is a possibility of some sort of joint administration. Then France will be, at any rate, one of the influential partners in such a condominium. Therefore, permit me to put the question again: will French influence then be favorable to Zionism?"

At this point there came to the fore the "classic" diplomat from whose vocabulary the words "yes" and "no" have been erased. Just like the stage Jew, he answered the question with a question.

"Hasn't France proved her sympathy for the Israelites sufficiently? Didn't our great revolution first pronounce the equality… ?"

"For all that, M. Le Ministre, we are sincerely and eternally grateful," I said, "but I've come from Russia and the Ukraine where six million Jews are wracked by one thought – what will happen to Palestine?" (I hope Heaven will forgive me those six millions wracked by one thought!)

He was silent for a moment and then asked, changing the subject in accordance with that same "classic" method, "What is the plight of the Jews in Russia now?"

"Worse than ever before," I answered curtly and precisely, because I, for one, do not belong to the "classic" school – and because I had already received an answer to what really interested me.

Gustave Hervé, kindly soul, still tried to help. He told the minister that a Jewish unit had been formed in Egypt.

"So I have heard," interrupted Delcassé, "but for Gallipoli."

"Yes, but they now want to organize a new corps for Palestine and they would be happy if this corps were included in the French Army."

"That is," I added, "provided the French Government is sympathetic to Zionism."

Delcassé rose, terminating the interview on a doubtful note: "It is altogether uncertain whether there will be a campaign in Palestine, and when, and who will lead it...."

That same day I sent a report to London with the following two conclusions: (a) France is already aware that she will not be allowed to annex Palestine; (b) The Government is not interested in Zionism.

In 1925, exactly ten years after this interview, I related this conversation to a French senator, a great friend of Zionism and one of those statesmen (there are many of them in France) who to this day regret that Palestine did not come under French jurisdiction. He shook his head regretfully. "The worst possible thing for a politician is to lack imagination. That was diplomacy of the time of Pepin the Short! Not to understand that a dream, once it is dreamed by millions, is in itself a great empire, not a whit weaker than France or England or Germany..."

I know now that later, after the creation of the Jewish Legion and after the Balfour Declaration, Delcassé himself admitted to Paul Cambon, the French minister in London, that he regretted the attitude he had adopted in that conversation. To me, now, this is something of a comfort: it is pleasant to know that not only did you fail, but the other and stronger fellow failed as well. At the time, however, this conversation was a great disappointment to me.

But my stay in Paris was not entirely bereft of positive results. Dr. Weizmann promised his assistance in my Legion activities; and a time came when he kept his promise.

Old Baron Edmond de Rothschild, the father of Palestine colonization, was enthralled with the news about the Zion Mule Corps.

"You must continue at all costs! See that it becomes a real Legion when the time of the Palestine Campaign arrives!"

And although deep down in my heart a small voice asked, "Why I? Why not you? Surely it is easier for you?" – I was thankful for his kind words. His son James, at that time still a sergeant in the French Army, who was lying wounded in his father's hospital, questioned me on the Legion idea, half acquiescent and half ironical in his manner; but later, in England, he often assisted me through his invaluable connections, and subsequently joined the Jewish Regiment himself and even conducted its recruiting campaign in Palestine.

Charles Seignobos, the famous historian, was then co-editor with Paul Painlevé, of the *Annales des Nationalités* a review which defended the cause of the oppressed minorities. He wrote a short note on the back of his visiting card to his friend, Mr. Henry Wickham Steed, then editor of the London *Times*. Of all the assistance I received in those difficult years, this little card proved to be the most powerful, for it opened for me the door not merely to a man of influence, but to a journalist. I have been a journalist ever since my youth and am not ashamed to admit that in my well-considered opinion, journalists are, will and must be the world's ruling caste.... However it was not until much later that I was able to use that slip of paper – and meanwhile, my Paris experience was a failure.

London: Again a failure.

At the War Office I was told that Lord Kitchener, then war minister as well as military idol of the British, was opposed to any kind of "fancy regiment" as well as to any offensive on Eastern fronts. I tried to meet Mr. Herbert Samuel, who was a member of the Asquith cabinet and who had already associated himself with Zionism; Weizmann, too, wanted to introduce me to him, but Sokolov and Tschlenov vetoed the idea – and they, not he, were members of the "Inner Actions Committee." Samuel had read in the *Jewish Chronicle* a lengthy report from

Egypt regarding the Zion Mule Corps, and asked them who and what I was. Dr. Gaster, Chief Rabbi of the London Sephardic community and a relative of Samuel, replied, "Oh, just a talker." Neither Sokolov nor Tschlenov protested.

I met the younger generation of English Zionists – Norman Bentwich, Harry Sacher, Leon Simon and others. Their idol was Ahad Ha'am. They laughed at my idea; some of them politely.

Copenhagen: a failure, and a break – with the Zionist Organization. In the summer of 1915 a session of the Greater Actions Committee took place. Delegates came from Germany, Russia, England and Holland. I was in Stockholm at the time, and not being a member of the Committee, I was not entitled to participate in the session.

But Dr. E. Tschlenov and Dr. Victor Jacobson sent for me, and at a private meeting in a hotel they, together with Hantke, tried to prove to me that the formation of the Zion Mule Corps had been a great mistake and that pressing onward with the agitation for a Legion would destroy Zionism. In my notebook I have several interesting observations of that meeting, which lasted three hours. Some of them sound somewhat comic now.

Dr. Hantke proved to me that two and two make four – and that therefore Germany would win the war (indeed, at that time the Russians were being badly beaten in Galicia). Dr. Jacobson showed me historically, statistically and economically that Turkey would never leave Palestine, and that on the contrary the near future would see a rising in Egypt, Algiers and Morocco.

"My friends," I said, "this discussion is useless. You come from Germany or from tottering Russia; but I have seen England, the French front, Egypt, Algiers and Morocco. You are utterly wrong: Germany will not win and Turkey will be driven into Anatolia. But why should we argue? I propose to compromise: you can declare that the Zionist Organization is neutral and washes its hands of all Legion plans. I shall leave the Zionist Organization officially and do my work as a private person; I shall not interfere with your work and you will let me alone."

But they *did* decide to interfere. The Actions Committee passed a resolution that all Zionists everywhere must oppose the Legion propaganda – and I suddenly found myself in a state of war with the entire Zionist Organization, almost alone.

Almost, but not quite alone. Never shall I forget that in that very Copenhagen, at the same time as this painful breach, I found the colleague who provided the support – at times a heroic support – which alone made it possible for us to endure the purgatory of the two ensuing years. Meir Grossman was living in Copenhagen as the correspondent of a St. Petersburg newspaper. I shall often have to refer to our common struggle.

And then in conclusion quite a sad chapter: Russia in the summer of 1915.

This was the last time I saw the country where I was born and had grown up. I spent three months there, visiting St. Petersburg, Moscow, Kiev and Odessa. Over everything hovered already the imminence of the end. The army had been driven out of Galicia; the Germans took Warsaw, and somewhat later, Riga. But it was not this which foretold the "end": it was the indifference with which it was all accepted. In the words of a friend who was an habitué of the night-spots: "In the morning paper you read, 'Bialystok has fallen,' and at night you see very gay officers with very prettily dressed young women at the Bear Club, the Villa Rohde, the Aquarium – hedged around with dust-covered bottles." Luxury the like of which we had never seen in Russia before was dazzling everywhere, and carefree, cheerful chatter poured forth about Lord knows what – mainly about the good fortunes of this and that well-born libertine with ladies (and men) of the aristocratic set: it was a continuous mud-bath involving the big names of the court nobility, of the financial and the literary world. Rasputin ruled the palace, deciding who was to be governor of Tomsk, who would command the southern front, who should treat the tsarevitch. In the inner apartments of the palace a lonely family, already tragic, was hiding from people; its strangely bourgeois life and mentality were being discussed freely and loudly by idlers in every restaurant. The picture one conjured up listening to all this gossip was depressing. A little, melancholy, sympathetic but deeply unkind epigone of ten different but equally degenerate Houses; his wife, a German in whose soul Prussian conceit mingled somehow with Russian mystic masochism; four colorless daughters who probably might have become nice young women but for the utterly provincial and uncultured atmosphere in which they were kept – and a sickly boy whose watery blood already refused to coagulate even at the slightest prick. A lonely family on whom the grand dukes, their own kith and kin, had long since turned their backs; blindly in love with each other, blind to the entire world, deaf to the rumble of impending ruin – and what is more, proud and content with their blindness and deafness. In the Duma: on one hand the Black Hundred of all shades who, after every new blow at the front, stuck out their chests and alertly stabbed the enemy on the map with their forefingers; on the other hand, the left-wingers of every description, perhaps the only people in St. Petersburg whose hearts really ached in these days – but they too comforted themselves with the wretched solace of the weak, repeating daily, "We told you so."

Among the Jews, as always at such times, there was a mixture of anguish and hope and hysterical restlessness. At the front the poisonous, treacherous hangman, a "Russian patriot" of Polish origin, Yanushkevitch, had run amok, hanging tens of Jewish "spies," driving out whole communities from towns and villages; hungry refugees, tattered and bare, crowded every railway station; examples of fine solidarity flickered by – old rabbis who refused to travel by cart but rather dragged along hundreds of miles with the crowd of exiles, young girls who waited through the night at the railway stations with parcels of food and clothing, because somewhere, somehow, they had heard that a train filled with refugees was arriving they knew not when, they knew not whence. Millions of good old Russian rubles for charitable assistance were given with the fine, great-hearted liberality which was once the pride of the Russian Jews. And at the same time, millions were earned through war profiteering, and millions wasted, on wives and other men's wives; and there was a continual waiting for something to happen – something, an earthquake of fortune, a great redemption; and a brilliant unprecedented flare-up of Zionist, almost messianic, dreams; and baptized Jews, and mixed marriages, and Hebrew in every railway carriage – and everywhere a timid whispering that it was time a self-defense was organized.

I saw all this as an onlooker. My Russian colleagues on the Moscow newspaper received me like a kinsman. But in Zionist St. Petersburg I was met with stony faces – while the Zionist leaders I did not meet at all. I was excommunicated: after twelve years of national activity I was suddenly anathematized and treated like an outcast. In Odessa, my home town, where not long before I had – quite undeservedly – been carried shoulder-high, I was now, on Sabbaths and Festivals, called a traitor from the pulpit of the Zionist synagogue, "Yavneh." I think that in the whole Zionist "older generation" there was only one man who had the courage to come to see me in daylight. That was Israel Trivus, with whom, in 1903, I had organized the first Jewish self-defense organization in Russia. He shook his head and said, "One should never save one's fatherland without an invitation."

I do not wish to offend anybody, but this boycott did not disturb me unduly. What did hurt me, however, was something absolutely indecent: my old mother, wiping away her tears, confessed to me that one of the best-known bosses of Russian Zionism, a good man with the solid reputation of a boor, had come up to her in the street and said to her point-blank, "Your son should be hanged."

She was deeply hurt. I asked her: "Tell me, Mother, what should I do now?"

And I shall ever remain proud of her reply: "If you are sure you are right, you must not give in."

The only exception was Kiev. There I was received like a brother, and especially by the local Zionist leaders, N. S. Sirkin, M. S. Mazor and Jonah M. Machover. The first two are no more. Many of the people whose names I have mentioned in these notes are no longer with us, but recording the loss of these two is exceptionally painful. Even among the first "recruits" of "old" Russian Zionism there were very few who possessed such gifts as the first, such profound wisdom as the second, or such purity of idealism as both of them. I never saw them again after that meeting in Kiev.

The Kiev people received me as one of themselves. They called a meeting, listened to my report, approved, encouraged me, gave me their blessing and promised to help as much as they could; and they kept their word. More than once when I was in difficulties in my work I sent a telegram to Kiev: "Help me out," and I always had my reply through the bank. It may sound very banal, but truly more precious to me than their material help was the recollection, in later years, of our cordial reunion and of the "good luck" with which they bade me farewell when I left.

Professor Manuilov, editor of the *Russkya Vyedomosti*, was at first opposed to my going abroad again. "Stay and work with us in Moscow," he suggested. "Why should you go to the West again?"

"Legion," I replied.

"If so, Godspeed," he said; and for the next two years, until the Bolsheviks closed it down, this old, honorable, liberal paper, the pride of the Russian Press, enabled me to live in London, to maintain my family in St. Petersburg – and to do as I pleased.

Chapter IV

Alone Against Everybody

On my way back to London I broke my journey at Copenhagen to see Grossman. He had no good news for me. The Zionists had opened an office in Copenhagen and had already dispatched circulars far and wide appealing for the prevention or stoppage of all propaganda for the Legion and for the boycotting of its initiators. As a result, several student groups in Switzerland had already adopted "heroic" resolutions against the Legion. We had gained only one new supporter: in the Hague, the capital of Holland, a response had come from a young man named Jacob Landau. He proposed the creation of a Press Agency which should propagate the Legion idea, and had begun to publish small articles and news items in this spirit in the Dutch newspapers. The Zionists, led by Mr. Nehemia de Lieme, had excluded him from their organization and had threatened to persuade the Dutch police to drive him out of the country as a foreigner who had abused his neutrality. He was not intimidated (this was the Jacob Landau who is today at the head of the Jewish Telegraphic Agency), and until the end of the Legion campaign he pursued this agitation in the neutral newspapers, which in those war years were rather influential in Central Europe.

We decided to establish a paper – the *Tribune*. During the past few years, traveling through Germany, Austria, Czechoslovakia and Rumania, I have found many people who still have in their possession a collection of those green booklets which Meir Grossman published in Copenhagen from 1915 to 1917. And these people told me that this was the "only honest word" a Zionist could hear in Central Europe in those days, to learn a little of the truth of the situation in Palestine, of the attitude of Turkey to Zionism, of the war orientation which should be worked out by the Zionist Organization.

It long remained a mystery to me how Grossman could maintain his paper. There was not much I could do to help him from London. I could not even assist him with the distribution of the *Tribune*: starting with the second issue, the British censor, in his wisdom, had prohibited the sale of the one and only pro-British organ in the Jewish press, on the pretense that it attacked the antisemitic policy of the Russian Government. I love the British, but no blunderer in the world can compete with an English bureaucrat when he lays his hands on something "exotic."... Later, however, I discovered the explanation of Grossman's miracle: he used to pay the printer out of his own salary.

In mid-August, 1915, I returned to London and found that the situation was completely unfavorable for my plan.

First, there was Kitchener's policy. His doctrine was a simple one: all efforts must be directed to the Western Front only; the East was not important. The British considered him a great strategist – though I heard, even during his lifetime, altogether different opinions, very pointedly and bitterly expressed, especially from experts. I must here repeat what I have already written about Delcassé: not everybody whom the Gentiles consider great is really great. Kitchener was a first-class soldier and an outstanding organizer; but a strategist is something entirely different. "Strategy" is the art of finding, in a large and far-flung front, the weak spot of the enemy. In addition, a strategist must possess that quality known as "imagination," and this

Kitchener did not have. He was, so to speak, a fine artillerist: there is the enemy line, this is the distance – bring your guns, or, if these are not enough, bring twice as many, and shoot! For this, too, talent and brains are required. But the brain of a strategist is of another caliber – his is the brain of the chess player. There came a time – much later – when even in the War Office they saw that Kitchener's strategy was stunted. Shortly before his death there began to grow in the army staff, in Parliament and in the press a strong body of feeling which favored a campaign on the Eastern Front. This section tried to show that that was the enemy's weak spot and that Turkey could be destroyed with little effort, thus dealing Germany a death blow, since the whole purpose of the war for Germany lay in conquering the East. Lloyd George himself was one of those who thought thus. But Kitchener would not, and could not, give in. I am certain that had he not died so tragically Lloyd George would have forced him to resign a few months later.

In the autumn of 1915, however, Kitchener was still the popular idol, and the idea of an Eastern offensive had been adversely affected by the disaster of the Dardanelles.

"A regiment for Palestine?" I heard on all sides. "Nobody is even thinking of an offensive in Palestine. We don't need it."

Then there were the Zionists. The organization in England was at that time even smaller and less influential than it is today. But the war had provided it with two first-class directors from the outside – Tschlenov and Sokolov. They were both opponents of the Legion idea, and this fact decided the general attitude even before any dispute arose. The only spiritual influence of any power in English Zionism was also unfavorable. Ahad Ha'am was living in England at the time, surrounded by a small circle of supporters, some of whom still declare today that we do not need a Jewish majority in Palestine and that we shall never attain it.

There were a few exceptions. Joseph Cowen and Dr. Eder supported me throughout. Indeed, it is to them that the idea of a Jewish battalion belongs: they agitated for it in the first months of the war – not particularly for Palestine, but in general. Naturally, they were unsuccessful, and their influence was weak compared with that wielded by Sokolov, Tschlenov and Ahad Ha'am.

In the true Jewish center, in Whitechapel, I found but one supporter: Mr. A. Beilin, a good writer, but uninfluential.

Dr. Weizmann was different. In Paris he had already declared himself a supporter of the Legion. In London we came still closer together. We even lived together for three months in a small house somewhere in a side street in Chelsea, a stone's throw from the Thames. He was in the first stages of work in the Government Laboratory on his well-known chemical discovery, which was later so important in cheapening the production of munitions and which brought him into touch with the then minister of munitions, Lloyd George. Though he worked eight to ten hours a day in the laboratory, he found time to take active steps in his political work, establishing new connections and influencing new powerful supporters. In those months we became great friends, and I hope that we shall remain so – even though the political struggle has driven us away from each other and will probably never bring us together again.

Dr. Weizmann was in favor of my plans, but he admitted to me honestly that he could not and did not care to make his own political work more complicated and difficult by openly supporting a project formally condemned by the Zionist "Actions Committee" and extremely unpopular with the Jewish population of London.

Once he told me, and it was very typical of him: "I cannot work like you, in an atmosphere where everybody is angry with me and can hardly stand me. This everyday friction would poison my life and kill in me all desire to work. Better let me act in my own way; a time will come when I shall find a means to help you as best I can."

Such a time did come, he kept his word, and I have not forgotten it. But then, in the autumn of 1915 and long afterward, his sympathy could find no tangible expression, nor could it alter the general atmosphere in which I lived – irritation and hostility from all sides.

The third and worst of the unfavorable factors was the Jewish youth itself. London's East End continued to enjoy life as usual, to the fullest extent. Healthy, replete, well-dressed young men thronged its broad sidewalks, restaurants, tea-rooms, movies and theaters every night: a separate isle inside England, divided from it by another and even deeper Channel. Their first reaction was not even hostile: it was just indifferent. If the soul of a collective group could be summed up in a formula, I would choose as typical of theirs Stolypin's famous words: "So it was, so it shall be." Palestine? We lived without it, didn't we? It means that we can continue to do without it. It has long been in foreign hands; it means that it can continue to remain so. There is no Jewish regiment: it means there won't be any. And, although we quietly relax in tea-rooms while English youth is dying in trenches, so far nobody interferes with us: it means we shall continue to be left alone. Not only was it impossible to make them realize the true situation; it was impossible even to trouble their placidity, make them afraid for their own tomorrow. Since today is quiet, it means that tomorrow also everything will remain as it was before. This kind of impressionism, based exclusively upon last week's experience, is an inveterate disease of the ghetto; but never before or after have I observed it in such quantities.

I suppose that Whitechapel was neither worse nor better than other immigrants' districts in any other city, but in the atmosphere of Whitechapel there was something else, besides – something unpleasant, of which other immigration centers are innocent. Whatever the faults of the American ghetto, it may still be proud, and rightly so, of its big heart and generous giving; it has the tradition (or at least the illusion) of a certain idealistic (or at least merely sentimental) attitude to the outside world, to both poles of the outside world – their hearts ache for the Jewish people, and they are proud of America. The ghetto of Paris is passive as far as Jewry is concerned, but it is at least sincerely and gratefully attached to France. The East End neither loves nor hates: the East End has no attitude at all either to countries or to classes. It may be different now, but then it was so. They said themselves: "Bring any idea to Whitechapel – it will turn sour, like milk in a closet."

There were exceptions, even brilliant ones, but they were like drops in the ocean.

I remember what one clever anarchist from Whitechapel told me about the soul of its people; his judgment was well-coined and full of bitter humor. It happened in the autumn of 1916. Grossman and Trumpeldor had already arrived, and together we tried in public meetings to convince the Jewish youth that the only decent way out of the situation was a Jewish Legion; and the youth answered us with clamor, abuse and scandals.

Mr. J., that anarchist, said to me after an especially stormy meeting, "How much longer do you intend to knock your head against the wall? You do not understand a thing about our boys. You explain to them they should do this thing 'as Jews,' that thing 'as Englishmen,' and that other 'as men.' Nonsense. We are not Jews. We are not Englishmen. We are not men. What are we? We are tailors."

I mention these bitter words only because in the final account the East End proved that it was worth its salt. It gave us first-rate soldiers, brave and tenacious; even the nickname "tailor" itself – "*schneider*" – gradually acquired in all our battalions a sort of honorary meaning, became the synonym of a real soldier who carries out his duty without complaining or bragging, exactly, strictly and quietly. Somewhere in the deepest recess of Whitechapel's soul there was a hidden source of responsibility, a forgotten kernel of self-respect, and when the hour of test and danger struck, it finally manifested itself in spite of everything. In the final account that anarchist was proved wrong, as probably always and everywhere those who criticize the masses are wrong – in the final account. But in the beginning, his diagnosis fitted like a glove: I don't know whose fault it was (maybe it was due to the hard-boiled coldness of their English environment), but in Whitechapel, precisely that nerve which connects the individual with the sum, the race, the land – with mankind – had become numbed. The only link with a collective entity they could still grasp was reduced to their trade: I am a merchant, you are a teacher, we are tailors....

The most amazing thing about them was their blindness to everything that went on behind the imaginary wall which divided them (or so they thought) from the rest of England. "Nobody interferes with us"...but my first steps in London showed me clearly all the symptoms of the storm about to break out, and precisely over the East End. In every room of the War Office, in the editorial rooms of every newspaper in London, from every aunt and cousin of my English landlady in Chelsea, I heard one and the same irritated complaint: our flesh and blood perish by the hundreds every hour, while those young men of yours entertain their girlfriends and play billiards. The press had already begun to ventilate cautiously the question of conscription – for the time being not for Whitechapel, but only for the English youth. One had to be asleep not to realize that the very next call would be for the undisturbed foreigners. Slumbering is pleasant, however, and people resent strongly the uncalled-for efforts of one who tries to rouse them.

Such was the main source of manpower on which my plans were established. I was almost alone: the Zionists had excommunicated me, and Kitchener said that there was no need for a Palestine campaign and that he did not want any "exotic" battalions.

I am not blind. I saw all this clearly, had calculated, weighed, checked and rechecked every factor. I cannot say that I reached the final conclusion without doubts and hesitations. On the contrary, the doubts were many, and there were many moments of despondency. Nevertheless, my conclusion was steadfast, and here it is, paragraph by paragraph.

Lord Kitchener is mistaken: England will have to fight on the Palestine front.

Another error of Lord Kitchener's: a Jewish Legion is not a fancy idea but an unavoidable necessity for England herself. The government will be compelled to create it, because the public opinion of England will force it to mobilize the East End – and a Jewish contingent for Palestine is the only form in which that mobilization can be carried out without provoking a worldwide scandal.

The Zionists are wrong. The Legion is a necessity for them also – and the time will yet come when they will crowd the streets of Whitechapel and applaud its triumphal march.

Whitechapel is also wrong: it will be "interfered with," and soon. The only way out for its youth is called the Legion. Serve they will – and will yet be thankful for the opportunity to fight for the Jewish cause.

"Everybody is wrong, you alone are right?" No doubt this question springs by itself to the reader's lips and mind. It is customary to answer this with apologetic phrases to the effect that I fully respect public opinion, that I bow to it, that I was glad to make concessions.... All this is unnecessary, and all this is untrue. You cannot believe in anything in the world if you admit even once that perhaps your opponents are right, and not you. This is not the way to do things. There is but one truth in the world, and it is all yours. If you are not sure of it, stay at home; but if you are sure, don't look back, and it will be your way.

Chapter v

How Politics Are Made

It would take too long and would be too dreary if I were to present a diary of the events of those two years – until the day in the summer of 1917 when the order for the creation of a Jewish Regiment was gazetted.

I shall only mention several episodes, some of them as stages on our way, others because of the figures that appear in them – figures many of whom played an important part in the events of the world, or in *our* world. In general, however, I consider this series of episodes to be an illustrated reply to the question which is very often heard these days at Zionist meetings: How can one "force" a government which is unwilling. By using threats? By beating one's fist on the table? By raising one's voice? No, my friends. When a government is "unwilling," remain quiet and cool; only – take no notice of negative answers. Go on, try again, recruit new adherents, no matter whether low or high – until the government is converted and is even pleased at having been "forced" to change its mind.

One cold and slushy winter evening, there was a knock at my door, and a young man, very poorly dressed, came in and handed me a grimy piece of paper. I recognized the handwriting on the paper as that of a friend who lived in Jaffa. The note was in Hebrew: "This is Harry First. You may trust him."

"I come from Palestine," said the young man. "The workers there have heard that you wish to raise a Jewish Regiment; so they told me to come to you and to tell you that they are with you and that you should not let yourself be intimidated. This is the first thing. Secondly: I am at your service. I speak Yiddish and English; I am a member of the Poale Zion, and know Whitechapel. What shall I do?"

"Settle in Whitechapel," I replied, "and talk to the youth."

He rose and went. And for two years Harry First agitated in Whitechapel, in workshops, in restaurants, in his committee and at meetings; one after another he sought out individual supporters, introduced them to me and then went on with his work. He became one of the best-known figures in Whitechapel; he was loved and hated. Hated for obvious reasons; loved because even opponents admired his quiet, sincere determination and his noble poverty. When the Legion came into being he went into khaki, quietly and conscientiously served his two years in Palestine, sought no honors, seldom even came to see me. Afterward he disappeared, and today I do not even know where he is. Perhaps somebody will show him these lines: Shalom, Harry First, one of those "unknown soldiers" by whom, and not by "leaders," history is made.

In Whitehall, whence Britain and half the world is ruled, the government had created a Propaganda Department; but I did not know it.

One day the Admiralty invited the correspondents of the foreign press to the naval base of Rosyth in Scotland – to view the British Home Fleet. Among those who accompanied us was the English journalist, Masterman. We talked about the Alexandria venture, of which he had heard, and I told him about my plans.

He said: "I now look upon everything from the angle of

propaganda. Your project is splendid propaganda material. Would you like to see Lord Newton about, it?"

"Who is he?"

"Minister of propaganda. Let me have the material. I will prepare a report for Lord Newton, and he will give you an appointment."

In England things are done leisurely; a few months later I shaved with more care than usual, climbed on top of an omnibus and went to Whitehall to see Lord Newton.

"Perhaps it is a good idea," he said, "and of course I have heard and read about the Zion Mule Corps. But what has it to do with my department, with propaganda?"

"One question: Do you place any value at all on the attitude of neutral Jewries?" I asked.

"Yes," he replied. "We are unfortunately not satisfied with the attitude of neutral Jews. Every week I see translations from the American Jewish Press.... I don't understand them. Is it our fault that the Russian regime is... h'm... h'm... not so modern?"

"It makes no difference whether it is your fault or not. Let us talk facts. A victory for you will strengthen the Russian regime, and that is a fact that England cannot evade. England can only counterbalance it."

"How?"

"There is only one thing that a Jew loves even more than he hates the Russian regime – Palestine! Only through a great love can you forget a great hatred – not otherwise."

"Does that mean that if the British Government issued a manifesto in favor of Zionism, then...?"

"Then the American Jews would say: Fine, but what is a manifesto without facts? At the beginning of the war a term was created – 'scrap of paper' – and this term has become sadly popular. A manifesto – certainly; but you must have facts, besides."

"What do you mean by facts?"

"A Jewish Corps which should participate in the conquest of Palestine."

"But nobody knows yet when we shall go to Palestine; and Lord Kitchener says never."

"A regiment is not the ricinus of Jonah." You may quote the Bible to an Englishman: he understands. "An army does not arise overnight. If it will be required next year, you must start work today. As for Lord Kitchener, many experts disagree with him."

"Tell it not in Gat," he replied, "but – I shall consider the matter and discuss it with my colleagues."

Cutting, fiery articles were published by the American Jewish newspapers against Russia in 1917. But the writers and editors themselves probably did not know how powerful they were in paving the way for the Balfour Declaration and for the Jewish Regiment.

Mr. Joseph King, a Liberal MP, made an inquiry in the House of Commons as to whether the Home Secretary was aware of the fact that "a Russian journalist" was making propaganda in Whitechapel to establish a Jewish Regiment and whether this journalist had any authority from the government.

I wrote him, "Sir, before you attack a man and his plans, hear his case."

We met in the National Liberal Club. When I entered the hall I saw that he was in conversation with an emaciated gentleman, possessor of a yellow and withered Torquemadan face – or perhaps semi-Torquemadan and semi-Mephistophelian. Mr. King nodded to me. The thin gentleman looked away. They parted, and Mr. King motioned me to a seat.

"My Whitechapel friends," he began, "have complained bitterly against you. They plead that a public and press agitation is beginning against those aliens who have not enlisted – and then you come and add fuel to the flames."

"Mr. King, tell me frankly, if I should disappear, would that agitation cease?"

"Unfortunately not," he replied. "I cannot deny that the public does not like to see young able-bodied men living among us, and yet..."

"Then, Mr. King, let us take it that my plan is bad; but tell me, do you see any other solution? Give me a way out. Do you want them to remain outside the army to the end? Do you want us to sit still and watch the growth of racial hatred in its most poisonous form – the hatred of people who must die against people who are permitted to live?"

"What you say is not new," he replied. "I have said the same to my Whitechapel friends. I have told them that it would be best if a large number of foreign Jews were to join the British Army together with our own boys."

"That is where you are mistaken. It is an unjust demand."

"Why?"

"Because there is a vast difference between your boys and those East End boys. Your boys are British; if Britain wins their people is saved. Ours are Jews; if Britain wins, millions of their brothers will still remain in purgatory. You cannot demand equal sacrifices where the hope is not an equal one."

"What do you want, then?"

"A compromise. In order to be just you can demand only two things from the foreign Jew: first, 'Home defense,' to protect Britain itself, because he lives here; second, to fight for the liberation of Palestine, for that is to be the *Heim* of his people. 'Home and *Heim*' – that is my war motto for your Whitechapel friends."

"You are a dreamer!" he said suddenly.

I pointed to the portraits hanging on the walls of the Club. "All dreamers!"

"I shall think the matter over," he said, "and discuss it with my colleagues. But I do not know whether it is worth while talking about it to my Whitechapel friends."

"It depends who they are," I replied.

"You have seen the most important of them, the gentleman to whom I was talking when you came in. He is not a Jew and is too old for military service, but he is deeply interested in the question. He is a Russian emigrant, Mr. Chicherin. Would you like to meet him?"

"No," I said.

"Remarkable!" he exclaimed. "I put the same question to him about you and he made the same reply. It's curious how you Russians hate each other. One feels that if Mr. Chicherin had just a little influence, he would derive the utmost pleasure from seeing you in jail – and I'm afraid that feeling is mutual."

"Certainly," I said with all my heart.

Of Mr. Chicherin (destined later to become Soviet commissar for external affairs) I had heard but little, then – he was not one of the "famous" emigrants. He was known rather because of the name he bore, for his uncle had been a great liberal publicist in the sixties and had written in favor of equal rights for Jews. But I knew that Mr. Chicherin was one of the real leaders of the agitation in Whitechapel urging the Jews to refuse any kind of military service. As for what Mr. King had said about "jail," he proved himself a prophet – but not for me.

❧

A letter with a London postmark: "I am here on convalescent leave from Gallipoli, Number So-and-so, Dover Street." Signed: "J. H. Patterson."

I had not yet seen Colonel Patterson. He had appeared among our volunteers in Egypt only after my departure from Alexandria for Brindisi, to keep my appointment with Rutenberg.

But I had heard a great deal about him. A Protestant, born in Ireland, he had formerly been an engineer by profession. As far back as 1896 he had been sent to build a railway bridge across the River Tsavo, somewhere in Africa not far from "our" Uganda. His fame had its birth at this bridge, for he is famous among a particular class of people – the big-game hunters of Europe and America. Patterson is the recognized prince of English lion-hunters.

On the Tsavo River his camp consisted of several hundred Swahili laborers; he was the only white man and the only one who could use a gun. In the neighborhood there appeared lions of the worst kind, known as man-eaters, for the reason that they despised all other edibles. Every night one would come into the camp, calmly choose his prey and carry him away into the dense forest. And one after another Patterson shot them, eight lions in all, and eight brown lion skins hang on the wall in his home. That was the origin of his book, *The Man-eaters of Tsavo*. My copy has printed on it: "Twenty-sixth edition." I know Englishmen who, when they set out on long journeys, take only two books with them – the Bible and Patterson's *Man-eaters*.

Through this book Patterson became acquainted with another big-game hunter – Theodore Roosevelt, whom he often used to visit.

After his Tsavo adventures came the South African War. Patterson joined the cavalry as a second lieutenant and rose to the rank of lieutenant colonel. Thereafter he dwelt for a long time in India, traveled over half the world's surface, lived through stormy and troublous days – a life which seems like a romance and not one of this prosaic century. Field Marshal Allenby, his one-time friend, calls him a "buccaneer": that is the name of those daring men who, over two hundred years ago, broke the power of Spain on the islands of the Caribbean Sea and helped – perhaps against their own will – to transform the Atlantic Ocean into an English lake.

And at the end of this adventurous career – he became the commander of the Zion Mule Corps in Gallipoli and of the Jewish Legion in Palestine: for which he received no gratitude from either Gentiles or Jews, but for which he declares he has no regrets.

I found him in his convalescent home – a tall, thin man of youthful middle age, with intelligent and cheerful eyes, the personification of what the English call "Irish charm," but with no hint of those "Irish" qualities of gloom and hair-splitting, the bane of Irish national life.... In addition, he was a great student of the Bible, for whom Gideon and Samson and David were living figures; and, fortunately, they sometimes represented to him the Jew of today.

"What is happening in Gallipoli?" I asked.

"A failure."

"The Zion Mule Corps?"

"A success. Excellent soldiers."

"Trumpeldor?"

"The bravest man I have ever seen. He is now in command of the corps."

From private letters I had received I knew exactly the troubles Patterson had had with our soldiers and with that obstinate holy man, Trumpeldor. But the Irish temperament forgot trivialities and said, "Excellent!"

"How is your plan progressing?" he asked.

"Lord Kitchener is against it."

"Realities are stronger than Lord Kitchener."

"Will you help me?"

"Of course. Come."

We drove to Westminster. In the large hall between the two Houses of Parliament he wrote something on a card and handed it to the attendant. Five minutes later a short man in khaki, wearing the brass cap of the General Staff, came out from the Commons side. He had a quiet, curt, somewhat dry manner of speaking – the manner of a very clever man who talks only about what he knows, and knows what he wants – and perhaps he wants things whose time will come only after many long years. Later, after the war, I heard it said of him in England, "A few inches taller, and he'd be premier." It is true that he is small, smaller even than Lloyd George, but I am not sure that this is always going to stand in his path. At that time he was only an ordinary MP; later he became Britain's colonial secretary.

Colonel Patterson introduced us. "Captain Amery. He knows of our project; give him the details."

I did. Six months later Mr. Amery was one of the most important members of Lloyd George's famous secretariat (known as the "kindergarten" to the elder political generation, who deplored the youthfulness of the members of this omnipotent group). Mr. King brought me into contact with a number of MPs, both Liberal and Conservative. And in the Propaganda Department there lay a thick file of reports, letters and press cuttings, marked "Jewish Regiment," with a note by Lord Newton: "Important."

❧

The press attacks directed against foreign Jews became every day more violent. Rich, assimilated notables, headed by Major Lionel Rothschild, made an appeal to East End Jewry, which contained all the usual ingredients: England gave you her hospitality, do your duty, and so forth. The first signatory of the appeal was Lord Swaythling: I was told that he was a most exalted person – but I must admit that until then I had never even heard of him.

The appeal failed to yield one single recruit to the army.

It was at that moment that Herbert Samuel, who was then home secretary, chose to intervene. As a Jew, he felt the situation especially keenly; but his own endeavors to find a way out of the impasse were rather clumsy. One day, for instance, he published a proclamation to the effect that any "Russian subject" of military age failing to enlist voluntarily in the British Army would be sent back to Russia.

Although a clever man, Herbert Samuel has this strange shortcoming: he is organically a doctrinaire; he does not see things with his eyes as they really are, but through some sort of conception of his own. What he sees is not real men as God created them but some abstract human creatures, constructed or rather construed by himself in his own, Herbert Samuel's, image and likeness. Having mentally produced such a personage, he then submits to him his arguments and demands with results that should not be difficult to imagine. When he later became high commissioner of Palestine, this characteristic of his caused considerable harm to ourselves, the Arabs and England's good name. It produced that same effect then in London, in the summer of 1916.

He probably expected that his attitude would produce an excellent impression upon English public opinion – a Jewish statesman so eager for the Jews to fight! – while the East End would become frightened and would rush to the recruiting offices. But psychology never was Mr. Samuel's forte. Whitechapel did *not* become frightened: not a single Russian "subject" was enlisted as a result of that proclamation; and the impression upon the British public was the worst possible. A Liberal peer – Lord Parmoor, if I remember rightly – said in the House of Lords, "If I were a Jew, I'd rather cut off my right hand than deliver a fellow Jew to Russian tyranny."

I took advantage of this little "misunderstanding" by calling together all the London correspondents of the Russian liberal press. In those years the British Government naturally set great store by the attitude of the Russian newspapers. There were about six of us, representing the leading progressive and radical dailies of St. Petersburg, Moscow, Odessa and Kiev. We conferred and decided to send a telegram to the war secretary, Lord Derby, informing him that the home secretary's latest move with regard to Russian émigrés in England was likely to create an undesirable impression among our liberal readers, and we should therefore appreciate an opportunity of talking it over with the minister.

Lord Derby decided that the best man to deal with this trouble would be the man who had started it: we received a telegraphed reply advising us that the home secretary, Mr. Samuel, would receive the Russian correspondents at the House of Commons.

That interview bore a very solemn character. Mr. Samuel brought along a small army of secretaries and clerks, with whom he silently but actively consulted during the proceedings by writing innumerable "chits." He sat at the head of a long table, while we journalists sat along both sides of it; our spokesmen stood up when they addressed him, and he, too, rose when he spoke.

We explained that the papers there represented covered about eighty per cent of Russia's reading public (which was quite true); that we were doing our utmost to keep up Russian society's war spirit by holding out the hope that England's democratic influences would, in the end, favorably affect Russia's regime as well; but that the proclamation, threatening to send back to Russia people who had left that country because of religious discrimination, cut right across our propaganda by suggesting that the influence acted rather the other way about.

"Gentlemen," Mr. Samuel asked, "what else can I do? Those Russian subjects refuse to enlist voluntarily, and resentment is growing against them. Can the government stand by in idleness, watching that resentment degenerate into downright antisemitism?"

And he looked straight at me and asked, "What is your opinion, for instance?"

"Sir," I said, "if you want those people to enlist, why appeal to their fear of Russia? It would be more dignified, and also more practical, to appeal to their own positive national feelings. The government should find out – it is not so difficult – whether there is not some aspect of the war and of victory which could promise them relief and redemption as Jews and offer them a form of service reconcilable with that side of their civil mentality."

He was very much impressed, he told us – but evidently not sufficiently impressed to suggest that he would himself bring that scheme, which alone was able to solve the problem, before the Cabinet. But his own "scheme" – the back-to-Russia threat – was officially withdrawn a few days after our interview, and the outcome of that incident could be summarized as follows:

Never get scared if a government takes a wrong decision: government decisions can be withdrawn just like private people's decisions.

If a situation which demands a solution has been left unsolved, that means that another attempt at solving it is due; so keep alert and push forward the solution you prefer.

During those three months I made another unexpected discovery, of such importance that even now it is often useful to me: I was amazed to see that the political influence of an assimilated Jew, however rich and respectable, is utterly negligible in matters pertaining to Jewish international policy. In these questions his own government will quite naturally take into consideration only nationally-minded Jews, even if, personally, they happen to be unknown foreigners and newcomers. Chaim Weizmann's example is brilliantly conclusive, and my own experience confirmed the fact.

When I settled in London I heard from all sides: "Without the assistance of the notables, the government will not even talk to you. First of all secure the support of the notables." I tried obediently. Not only did they withhold their support; on the contrary they warned me openly that they would obstruct my efforts. The only thing left to me was to go and knock at the doors of government offices myself – and then I found out that success depended least of all on the attitude of the notables. During all my negotiations I do not remember one single instance of someone in authority asking me, "What is Sir Isaac So-and-so's opinion on this matter?" I do not claim of course that the notables were all wrong, while we the foreign nationalists were right. The explanation is much simpler. The assimilated Jew has nothing to "offer": he has once and for all identified himself with the native population. His loyalty is guaranteed – and it is perfectly logical that in serious situations the government considers him as a most honorable but entirely free appendix to the nation to which he has assimilated himself. Not so the nationalist: the Jewish sympathies which he offers to enlist are no free addition. The government may value them or not, this is a matter for itself to decide; but these sympathies can be obtained only subject to certain definite conditions. That is why the assimilationist is received with courteous smiles while the nationalist is being negotiated with.

As I already mentioned, it was that "donkey battalion" from Alexandria, ridiculed by all wits in Israel, which opened before me the doors of the government offices in Whitehall. The minister of foreign affairs in St. Petersburg wrote about it to Count Benkendorf, the Russian ambassador in London; the Russian embassy forwarded reports on it to the British Foreign Office; the chief counsellor of the embassy, the late Constantine Nabokov, who afterward succeeded the ambassador, arranged for me meetings with British ministers, the American ambassador, Mr. Page, the French ambassador, Paul Cambon – and all that thanks to the eight months which Trumpeldor and his six hundred muleteers spent under fire in Gallipoli.

The Near Eastern Department of the Foreign Office, which dealt with all the questions relating to Palestine, was headed by that old friend of the Zionist cause to whom Dr. Weizmann and the founders of the Legion owe so much: Sir Ronald Graham. But his first contact with Zionism dated back to the days when, in his capacity as "adviser to" the ministry of the interior in Egypt, he received in Alexandria a delegation which was seeking to organize a battalion of refugees from Palestine.

Chapter VI

Between the Barracks and the War Office

By the autumn of 1916 it was clear to everybody that if a scandal was to be avoided and Jewish honor maintained, Whitechapel must join the ranks. Conscription had already been introduced in England. Many young men, complete strangers to me, used to come to Chelsea – a distance of several miles – and ask, "What shall we do? It is becoming unpleasant to look even the most sympathetic of Englishmen in the face. Is there any hope of the government's forming a Regiment for Palestine?"

The government, however, did not want to do so yet. Kitchener had gone, but his spirit still reigned at the War Office, and the opponents of an Eastern offensive were still the most influential section of the General Staff.

At a consultation of friends we decided that the time had come for a new, completely open attempt to place before both the government and public opinion a *fait accompli*. It was our plan to collect the signatures of young men for the following declaration:

"Should the government create a Jewish Regiment to be utilized exclusively either for Home Defense or for operations on the Palestine front – I undertake to join such a Regiment."

The slogan of the campaign was to be "Home and *Heim,*" and if we could obtain a sufficient number of signatures, a petition was to be presented to the government. The campaign was to be carried through entirely with private means, without any official assistance whatever. Joseph Cowen placed the necessary sums at our disposal.

I summoned Grossman from Copenhagen. On the eve of his arrival we issued the first number of a daily paper in Yiddish, *Unsere Tribune* (Our Tribune), of which he was to be chief editor: it featured an editorial bearing his signature (I wrote it, but Beilin, a master of Yiddish, carefully corrected my style so as not to disgrace Grossman). The chief contributors were Beilin, Pinsky and Kaiser. The first two already enjoyed a certain reputation as Yiddish and Hebrew writers, and the latter proved himself a very witty feuilletonist, although practically a newcomer to journalism. The technical organization of the campaign was undertaken by Harry First and Isaac Arshavsky, a young engineer from Russia: the latter came to one of our meetings just to listen, became converted at once to our ideas, and from that day placed at our disposal his very real capacities for organization, as well as his broad shoulders and impressive muscles. Both these characteristics proved most useful. A dozen young men worked under First and Arshavsky.

Several days later Trumpeldor arrived. His Zion Mule Corps had long been demobilized, after the failure of the Gallipoli campaign.

Two days after our first appeal appeared in the streets of Whitechapel, Soho and other Jewish quarters, Mr. Herbert Samuel sent for me.

"We are really grateful for your initiative," he said. "Can the Home Office help you in any way?"

"Only in one way," I answered. "Issue an official statement to the effect that, if a thousand signatures are collected, the government will form a 'Home and *Heim* Regiment.' If you do that, I am certain of success. If not, skeptics and opponents will not hesitate to brand the whole campaign as a 'trap' to catch volunteers who will be drafted to English battalions and sent to Flanders – and this will seriously hinder my work."

"I cannot issue such a statement. It does not rest with me alone. It is for the whole cabinet to decide. And you know that many Jews – particularly the Zionists – are strongly opposed to the formation of a Jewish regiment."

"My friends and I are just as strongly opposed to Whitechapel Jews serving in other battalions for the benefit of other nations. The obligation which we propose they should undertake is perfectly clear: only 'Home and *Heim*.' But without an official statement from you I cannot guarantee success."

"Can I help you in any other way, perhaps?" he asked.

I replied in the negative. And I say frankly that later I bitterly regretted that proud but unpractical reply. It was due to the old habit of all Russian liberals to view "authorities and officials" as unclean elements, from whom a decent person should not accept any assistance whatever. I had forgotten that such an attitude was absurd in England. One form of assistance I should have accepted and even demanded from the government: maintaining the peace at our public meetings.

Our campaign lasted a month and resulted in complete failure. We obtained altogether three hundred signatures – and Whitechapel life in those days was one interminable tumult. Our first meeting passed off quietly, for our opponents were afraid that there were police hidden somewhere in the hall, as was usually the case at recruiting meetings. But when they saw that we had adopted no such tactics, they came along to the second meeting armed with whistles. They were few in number – perhaps thirty in all – but well organized. Always and everywhere – in Whitechapel, Soho, Stamford Hill, Notting Hill – we saw the same thirty faces. And thirty noise-makers, as everybody knows, are a strong force when their purpose is simply to make a meeting impossible; more so, when the other side refuses on principle to call in the police and cannot permit itself the luxury of breaking thirty heads – for we had to keep the peace at all costs. We held out stubbornly, but the atmosphere of failure had already been created in the first week.

I hold no brief for Whitechapeldom, but justice demands that it be said that Whitechapel was not altogether to blame. Whitechapel was fully prepared to give us a hearing. All the more serious-minded elements, young and old, already understood that some positive solution had to be sought and that it was impossible for them to "have their cake and eat it." But how could they believe that our solution was a practical one? From the official Zionist side they had it dinned into their ears continually throughout the campaign that we were deceiving both ourselves and them, that the government would never permit the formation of a Legion, that the whole campaign was – as I had warned Mr. Samuel – a "trap." We had no official sanction for our plan. On this field of suspicion and doubt it was not difficult for a band of opponents to create an atmosphere of terror, to intimidate every young man who was only beginning to think seriously about our proposal, and frighten him into believing that he was a traitor, that he was dragging his brothers away, not to Palestine but to Flanders. And this band was well organized. The hand that pulled the strings, though it remained hidden itself, pulled them skillfully: it was the hand of Mr. Chicherin.

After four weeks we decided to close the campaign and to stop publishing the paper. Grossman returned to Copenhagen, and I made a sacred vow: that next time (for there will still be a "next time"), you, my dear friends, will not be able to make your noise, and the Chicherins will remain harmlessly quiet.

Exactly one month after this failure, the first nucleus of the Jewish Regiment was created.

One morning I received a visit from Trumpeldor. He brought me a note saying: "We arrived yesterday. There are 120 of us. Come to see us at barracks N. Nissel Rosenberg."

"Who is Nissel Rosenberg?"

"Don't you remember him from Gabbari? He was one of the best workers there, and later one of my best sergeants."

These 120 former soldiers from the Zion Mule Corps volunteered again into the army. They had had an eventful journey from Alexandria, striking a mine somewhere near Crete, but finally managed to reach their destination, London. Now their main worry was to be assigned to the same battalion, and not to be scattered in different camps. Their sergeants in the barracks, who took an instant dislike to the fancy group, assured them that they certainly would be separated.

Thanks to Patterson's and Amery's efforts they were all placed in the same battalion ("20th London") and formed into a separate company.

"Here you have your nucleus," Amery said to me. "If you only know how to make use of it, you need have no fears about the result. Feeling in favor of a Jewish Regiment already exists, both in the government and among the British public; and everything depends on this nucleus. Your whole plan must stand or fall by this small company of Zionist soldiers."

He was right. I myself knew that the feeling had been created. A lively correspondence regarding the Legion plan was already being carried on among the War Office, the Foreign Office, the Premier's Secretariat, where Captain Amery helped, and the Russian Embassy, where I found a staunch friend in First Counsellor Constantine Nabokov. Mr. King brought me into touch with the leading Liberal journal, *The Nation,* and Dr. Weizmann introduced me to the editor of the *Manchester Guardian,* C. P. Scott, then probably the most respected of all English journalists, and friend and teacher of Lloyd George. In both newspapers leading articles favoring the Legion had already appeared.

Most important of all, however, was the support of the London *Times.* At that time Lord Northcliffe was at the pinnacle of his power; a word of the *Times* was law. And the editor of the all-powerful newspaper was Henry Wickham Steed, to whom the French historian,

Seignobos, had given me an introductory letter. I had long before made use of it and was already well acquainted with this man, one of the three cleverest Englishmen I have ever met – a man of profound culture, who had spent half his life in various European countries and had been a personal friend of Theodor Herzl. In the *Times*, therefore, there had also appeared a leading article advocating the formation of a Jewish Legion. After this article appeared, even the most determined of our Jewish opponents looked crestfallen and said to me, "Of course, if the *Times* is on your side..."

Amery was right: everything now depended on the small Jewish company of the twentieth battalion of the London Regiment. This company was the right kind of seed; it was for us to make a tree of it.

I journeyed to Haseley Down, near Winchester, where the "20th London" was in training, introduced myself to Lieutenant Colonel Assheton Pownall and asked him whether he would accept me for service in the Jewish company. I related to him the story of our struggle and its purpose. He wished me luck, said, "Come along," and invited me to have lunch in the officers' mess. Later I was sorry I accepted: it was most unpleasant to stand to attention before young men with whom only a month ago I had drunk beer and exchanged merry jokes.

Then Trumpeldor and I sent a formal petition to Mr. Lloyd George, proposing to the War Cabinet the formation of a Jewish Legion for Palestine. It was Captain Amery's idea, who himself corrected the draft of the petition. The day before I became a private, while I still enjoyed the status of a free citizen from abroad (it was, I think, January 21, 1917), we signed together this document which Captain Amery undertook to hand over to the premier personally.

As a finale to my journalistic work – soldiers not being permitted to write on war questions – I handed to the printers a day before my going to the recruiting office, the manuscript of a book entitled *Turkey and the War*. The main ideas of the book were: that the war would be fruitless if Turkey were not partitioned; that Palestine should be annexed to the British Empire, and that the most important war front was in the Near and Middle East.

From the printers I proceeded to the recruiting office and received the "King's Shilling" – to be exact two shillings and sixpence – for my first day as a soldier.

I have mentioned the name of Mr. Steed. He deserves a more intimate introduction, for he played an important part not only in the history of the Legion but also in that of the Balfour Declaration. A month before the second of November, 1917, when the assimilationists, with Lord Swaythling at their head, made a final attempt to prevent the Government from making the pro-Zionist pronouncement, Mr. Steed replied to them in a shattering editorial. The *Times* had spoken....

As a young man, H. W. Steed had been a correspondent of the *Times* in Vienna, and there he had become acquainted and friendly with Herzl. He understood the mentality of Zionism as few Christians can understand it – the inner, spiritual, anti-assimilation aspect, just as incisively and deeply as the Herzlian thirst for political statehood. Naturally – as with any non-Jew who "talks like a Zionist" – many Jews accused him of antisemitism. This tendency among my fellow Jews – to see a Haman in every Gentile who permits himself to tell a "Jewish" anecdote (and his anecdote is usually a sugary compliment compared to those we tell against ourselves) – has always been completely incomprehensible to me. Mr. Steed spoke of Jews just as a Zionist would speak. He considered assimilation a veneer, he believed in the power of the Jewish people (in his book, *The Hapsburg Monarchy,* he opens the chapter on Austria's minorities with the phrase, "The most important of them is the Jewish nationality"); he spoke with moving, respectful earnestness of Herzl's ideals. And he crystallized his friendship in real, influential service at the greatest moment of our new history.

My barrack-room impressions would not make interesting reading. It is enough to say that I served like any other private, only I was not as young or as slim as the others. At first, when my arms ached from the anti-typhus injections, I used to sweep out the barracks and wash the tables of the Sergeants' Mess. ("Very well washed," Jewish Sergeant Blitstein told me laughingly. "If you like I'll ask the colonel to give you a permanent appointment to wash the tables at our Mess.")

This Ephraim Blitstein, a Russian Jew who had become, Lord knows how, a policeman in Alexandria, used to maintain order in our barracks at Gabbari; he was a splendid fellow who loved a joke, genial and cynical, as fat people often are.

Very soon I was transferred to the "Russian N.C.O. Class," not on account of my own qualifications but only by the colonel's grace.

My comrades in the Jewish company, however, were interesting. In an earlier chapter I told of the troubles at Gabbari. Here the number of men was smaller, but they were no less variegated. The majority, of course, came from Russia – and among them were three or four *gerim* (proselytes), with fair hair and blue eyes and a very good Hebrew pronunciation. One of them had come from Astrakhan, on foot through Mesopotamia to Jerusalem. At the close of the Sabbath he would make himself as drunk as a Volga peasant and then lie in a corner reading Psalms out of an old Hebrew prayer-book. There were seven Caucasian Jews from Georgia, with long names all terminating in *shvili*. It was a joy to hear English sergeants calling the roll in the morning: "Panikomoshiashvili?" – "Present!" The seven Caucasians were tall, handsome and strong – the strongest men in the battalion – quiet, modest and polite to each other, to their neighbors and to their elders: one of them wanted to take away the broom from me when I had been ordered to sweep the room. Another, Sepiashvili, was later the first man in the Legion to be decorated for bravery under fire. There were also a few born in Egypt, with whom I had to talk Italian or French. Two Daghestan Jews and one Crimean discussed their secrets in some Tartar dialect. And with one of them – he was a Christian Greek, and to this day I do not know how he managed to come to us – I found it utterly impossible to carry on conversation: I can struggle through seven languages; he knew three – but they were not the same.

Not all of them remained with us to the end. I have no idea what brought half of them to the army: perhaps the pressure of a consul, perhaps the urge of hunger, perhaps the lust for adventure, perhaps the general chaos of wartime, when one does not always know what one is doing. That half had no connection with Palestine. We soon rid ourselves of them – giving them to labor battalions, demobilizing them or sending them back to Alexandria. With the coming of spring there were left altogether about sixty – but these sixty were genuine. We had a great deal of trouble even with these – especially when the tidings of the Kerensky revolution came and there was still no Jewish Legion.

One fine morning, twenty of them refused to go out on parade and "presented an ultimatum"; in the army this meant "mutiny." Hours of persuasion on my part and the infinite patience of the colonel were necessary to prevent the danger of a court-martial, and I had to obtain the permission of the colonel for a representative of theirs to accompany me to London to Nabokov (who was acting ambassador after Benkendorf's death). Nabokov assured him that his information was that a Legion would soon be formed and that liberated Russia expected them to continue the heroic struggle which they had begun in Gallipoli.

But despite these troubles, the men were genuine. As there were now only sixty of us, we ceased being a company and became a platoon. But this "Platoon Sixteen" was the true nucleus from which the Jewish Legion grew; and in the Legion itself these former mule-drivers eventually played the part of backbone veterans, the indispensable framework of the structure.

In the meantime, Amery (Major Amery by then) managed to lay before the War Cabinet that "Jewish Legion" petition which

Trumpeldor and I had signed on the eve of my enlisting. The War Cabinet considered the petition, approved the principle and instructed the war secretary, Lord Derby, "to discuss the details with the signatories." I was on Passover leave in London, staying at my old Chelsea rooms; it was there, one bright April morning, that a messenger from the War Office brought me a hand-written letter signed by General Woodward, "Director of Organization." The general wanted Mr. "V.J." to be so kind as to call at the War Office at 2 P.M. that very day, the purpose being an interview with Lord Derby. "Sir," the letter began.... Obviously neither the general nor the war secretary suspected that the "Sir" was a full private in a British infantry battalion. Trumpeldor and I held a regular war council. What should we do? "When they see me in my uniform, won't they faint, both the minister and the general, before so unheard-of a prospect as a political consultation between such unequal partners?" I was all for asking Trumpeldor to replace me, but he felt rather doubtful about his English oratory. We compromised by deciding to go together. At two o'clock sharp, at the door of Room 215, War Office, we handed in our visiting cards and were asked to come in at once. I summoned all the resources of my civil and military courage, squared my shoulders and marched right in, cap on as per regulations; halted, saluted and introduced Trumpeldor and myself.

All honor to the general: though his face betrayed a high degree of astonishment, he did not show any of it in his words: just said, "Oh yes, I'll tell the war secretary," and walked out with eyes averted. But he stayed with the war secretary a full five minutes and more. Trumpeldor winked and whispered, "Now it is they who are holding a war council."

At last the general emerged from the sanctuary and invited us to follow him. Now, thank goodness, I could take off my cap, the war secretary being a mere civilian. I liked Lord Derby: a country squire of the grand ancient style, florid and tall and generously built, the classical (though now so rarely met) John Bull type with the "county" mannerisms of droppin his g's; and quite jolly and friendly. We all sat down, the general in a corner, stiff and wooden-looking as per regulation.

"The prime minister," Lord Derby said, "wants me to ask you for details of your Jewish unit scheme."

I rolled off the "details" automatically. By that time, I could have done it half-awake.

"I see," he said. "Now another point: do you anticipate a large number of volunteers?"

Trumpeldor answered him with true soldierly precision: "If it is to be just a regiment of Jews – perhaps. If it will be a regiment for the Palestine front – certainly. If, together with its formation, there will appear a government pronouncement in favor of Zionism – overwhelmingly."

Lord Derby smiled charmingly and said, "I am but a war secretary."

Trumpeldor smiled disarmingly and remarked, "I was but trying to answer your Lordship's inquiry."

"I see. Now the third question: I understand that, in the Twentieth Battalion of the London Regiment, there is a platoon of Zionist soldiers who served with the Zion Mule Corps in Gallipoli?"

"Yes, sir," I reported, "Platoon Sixteen – my platoon; and Captain Trumpeldor was their O.C. in Gallipoli."

The minister and the general looked at each other, then both looked at Trumpeldor, evidently noticing for the first time his parade-ground carriage and his dead left sleeve; and the minister nodded slightly in recognition, while the general stiffened even a little more.

"What would you think preferable," Lord Derby continued, "to train your platoon as N.C.O. instructors for the Jewish Regiment, or to send them, at the disposal of Sir Archibald Murray, as guides for any eventual operations in the South of Palestine?"

(British troops, by then, had already crossed the Sinai Desert; General Murray, G.O.C. Egyptian Expeditionary Force, was preparing for the attack on Gaza.)

Trumpeldor said, "So far as I know my former soldiers, there are hardly any who would be good as guides for Palestine; General

Murray will easily find much better ones. But they would make excellent instructors."

General Woodward intervened: "But weren't they a transport unit in Gallipoli? This will be an infantry unit."

"Colonel Pownall," I reported, "is very pleased with their progress in all manner of infantry drill; and besides, they speak fourteen languages among them, and this may come in most useful."

"Never imagined," said the minister, "there were fourteen languages under the sun."

He laughed most heartily; so did Trumpeldor; but the general didn't, so I thought I, too, had better abstain. I "reported" instead: "Yes, my Lord, there are, and in order to understand Jews, that's not enough, either."

"Well, I thank you," said the war secretary in conclusion. "As to the name of the Regiment, its badges and all that – General Geddes, Director of Recruitin', will send for you one of these days and talk it over."

And we went.

Next morning I was back in camp, and reported the conversation to Colonel Pownall. He assured me it was a breach of all the traditions of the British War Office and the first time in history that such an adventure had happened to a private soldier.

Yet the immortal gods do not like a man to get giddy with pride, even if he has just established a record. My pride was humbled on the same morning. My barrack-room neighbors had gone on parade, but I stayed behind, as my leave was still on, to admire and fondle no less a treasure than the advance copy of my own book, *Turkey and the War,* just then delivered by the mail-corporal. That was the book where I proved to the hilt that Turkey must be divided, and why, and who should get each part of the spoils. I simply loved the red cloth cover, I even patted it as if it were my first-born baby's head, and fell dreaming optimistic dreams about this baby's eventual conquests, the tremendous influence it was going to have on all military experts, smashing the late Lord Kitchener's "Westerners" school to smithereens, and definitely ensuring the triumph of Mr. Lloyd George's school of "Easterners."... Suddenly the orderly officer burst into the deserted barrack-room – a very young and very red-haired first lieutenant – preceded by his orderly sergeant. I sprang to attention. His eagle eye swept over the four walls; he frowned, and called out: "Halloa, that man with the glasses – open up!"

"Open what, sir?" I inquired.

"The windows, you bloody fool."

Chapter VII
Victory

Major Amery's activity did not flag, and I had one interview after another. Almost every second day I had to go to London from Winchester. This earned me a comical reputation in the Legion. The English sergeants refused to take me seriously as a soldier. When we had to run up to transfix the sack of straw which represented the enemy, and we were supposed to pierce it exactly in the "heart," my bayonet would pierce its "stomach." The sergeant would say, "Not so good for the front, but good enough for Whitehall." And on parade, when an orderly would be seen from afar doubling up in our direction with a brown envelope in his hand, the sergeant would say, "I suppose it's another telegram for Mr. Jug-of-whiskey." This was the accepted pronunciation of my name, being easier, having a pleasant sound reminiscent of God's good things, as well as being a recognition of my modest though decided tendencies toward anti-prohibition.

"We shall have to give you some rank," Colonel Pownall said to me. "The R.S.M. [the real chief, the Pope, the King of the Battalion!] says that you are a good musketry instructor."

"Yes, sir," I replied modestly, "I can't shoot well because of my eyes, but I know how it ought to be done."

There was one obstacle, and that was that there was no vacancy on the payroll. But finally he made me an unpaid lance-sergeant. I was not much concerned at receiving no pay, for I still sent occasional articles to Moscow, for which the good paper paid.

My friend Ginsberg, the London representative of "Carmel," sent me ten bottles of wine; these I presented to the Sergeants' Mess, where I sat like a lord at the same table which but six months earlier I had washed so well. Unfortunately, my successor at the washing job was not as talented as I had been.

Of the interviews I had in those days I have only short notes in my notebook, some of them undecipherable, for I was far too occupied to keep a diary.

The most important of these was one I had with General Smuts, the South African premier, who was in London at the time for the sessions of the War Cabinet. In those years he played an important part, not so much because of the assistance the little dominion could render in the war as because of his personality. Like General Botha, he had, twenty years earlier, been one of England's greatest enemies in the Boer War. His British patriotism, therefore, possessed the moral value of a manifestation of goodwill toward the British Empire. Moreover, Smuts was a deeply cultured man, educated at the Universities of Holland, Heidelberg and Cambridge, and a fine thinker and writer. He was a Zionist of the caliber of Balfour or Robert Cecil – one of those who considered the Balfour promise the finest heritage of the war. His presence in England greatly strengthened the pro-Zionist side in the War Cabinet. Smuts looked forty, though he must have been older – a lovable personality of the Continental type who spoke English almost like an Englishman but with a Dutch accent even more guttural than Yiddish.

He questioned me on all the details of the Legion plan. I made a note of one of his remarks: "That Jews should fight for the Land of Israel is the finest idea I have heard in my life."

At the conclusion he asked me a great deal about Russia. It was already known that the Army and the State were crumbling. I have in my book two observations which I noted. I do not know which of us made them, but I think it was he.

"Russia may fall and the Germans believe it will help them; but Samson destroyed more of his enemies at his death than in his whole lifetime."

"Kerensky is a holy man, but he is a lawyer, which means that he regards the world as one great tribunal of justice where the one who has the best arguments wins. As a result he is continually arguing. But his opponents are not depending on arguments; they are collecting dynamite."

Most important of the other meetings I had was the one with General Geddes, the director of the Recruiting Department (after the war he became British ambassador in Washington). Together we finally decided on the name of the Legion – "Jewish Regiment," plain and simple. The uniform was to be the ordinary English one but with a colonial mark like that of the Boy Scouts; the insignia, a Menora with the Hebrew word *kadima* (meaning both "forward" and "eastward") and a blue-white mark on the collar. One month later, thanks to the efforts of the assimilationist plutocrats, nothing of all this remained; and it was not until 1919 that we were given a Jewish name and Menora insignia.

"Who will be commander?" asked General Geddes. "Have you a Jewish nominee?"

A difficult question. In my pocket there lay a letter from Patterson, who was serving in Dublin at the time. He wrote: "It is my honest opinion that you should find a Jewish colonel. I would be happy to lead Jewish soldiers again; but justice and your national interests demand that this honor should be given a Jew."

Correct. But where was a Jew to be found?

In the group of assimilationists, of which Major Lionel Rothschild was the leading figure, we might have been able to find somebody. But in what sense could they be described as Jews? To me, "Jew" represents an honorable title, not an accident of birth. Among all the Jewish officers I got to know in London, only one regarded my work like a Jew – Major Schonfield. James Rothschild had been transferred from the French Army to the Canadian, but he was still only a lieutenant. Eliezer Margolin, who had been in my thoughts ever since our first days in the Gabbari camp in Alexandria, was somewhere on the Flanders front with his Australians. Of Colonel Fred Samuel I had not even heard at the time. But with all my feelings of respect to every one of these men, I considered then, and consider still today, that this historic privilege had been faithfully won by another: by the man who had not been ashamed to undertake the leadership of the Mule Drivers and who had converted them into a corps for which the war minister had profound respect; the man who in hospital and convalescent home had us ever in his thoughts, aiding us with his pen, writing his book, *With the Zionists in Gallipoli,* the man who believed in us when we were laughed at and ridiculed. "I remember the affection of thy youth…thy following me in the wilderness, in a land unsown."

"There is only one nominee," I said. "Even though he is not a Jew, he must be our colonel and I hope that one day he will be our general: Patterson."

Trumpeldor had already left London. He had pleaded to be accepted as an officer in the battalion in which I was serving with his former men. He was prepared to renounce his rank of captain and to become a second lieutenant; he would probably have agreed to be a non-commissioned officer, but the fact that he had only one arm prevented this from being even discussed. As for giving him officer's rank, the bureaucrats discovered a hundred different excuses, one of them perhaps with some justification – foreigners are prohibited from being officers in the British Army. Trumpeldor heard the decision, smiled and said, as usual, "*En davar.*"

He decided to go to Russia.

"What will you do there?" I asked.

He had two gigantic projects. In the first place he was certain that, with Boris Savinkov as minister of war in the Kerensky Government, permission could be obtained to mobilize a Jewish Army – not a Legion, but an army of one hundred thousand or more. This army would go to the Caucasian front and break its way through Armenia and Mesopotamia to Transjordan.

"And secondly?" I asked.

I shall never forget his answer to my question. He made his reply to me in a little room, gloomy and badly lit; to the Jewish people he gave his reply on the hills and in the valleys of Palestine. The people, too, will never forget his reply. His first plan was ruined by the Russian conflagration; the second he carried through. I did not write down his words. But it was not necessary: they echo in my ears even now. In that semi-dark little house of his in Chelsea, in midsummer, 1916, he propounded to me the simple and glorious idea of "*Hehalutz.*"

"What does it mean?" I asked. "Workers?"

"No. My conception is much broader. They must be workers as well, but not only that. We shall require people who are 'everything,' everything that Palestine will need. A worker has his worker's interests, a soldier has his ideas about caste, a doctor or an engineer his habits. But among us there must arise a generation which has neither interests nor habits. A piece of iron without a crystallized form. Iron, from which everything that the national machine requires should be made. Does it require a wheel? Here I am. A nail, a screw, a girder? Here I am. Police? Doctors? Actors? Lawyers? Teachers? Water-carriers? Here I am. I have no features, no feelings, no psychology, no name of my own. I am a servant of Zion, prepared for everything, bound to nothing, having one imperative: Build!"

"There are no such people," I said.

"There are."

I was mistaken. The first of them was sitting before me. He was himself a lawyer, a soldier, a farmer. He went to Tel Hai to seek work with the plow, found his death with a rifle, said "*En davar*," and died immortal.

Soon after my interview with Lord Derby, Colonel Pownall was ordered to start an instructors' class in our platoon. At its head he placed one of his sergeant-majors, a Jew named Richard Carmel, and myself. Carmel was a young man who had received a thorough English education. He hailed from somewhere in Wales, where there are few Jews, and knew but a few words of Yiddish. But from the beginning he "fell in love" with our boys and slowly with the Legion idea. He was, too, one of the finest instructors the British Home Army possessed.

I have pleasant memories of those summer months. People hear of the London fogs and do not know that England is in many respects the most beautiful country in Europe, with its many streams, little woods, soft hills and villages that look like postcard landscapes, and green, green as no other country on God's earth. The Hampshire Downs around Winchester, where we had our camp, is a quiet paradise. We spent our days on the Downs learning those portions of the soldier's lore that my comrades lacked. They did not lack much. The whole battalion used to talk with amazement of their shooting and bayonet exercises. It remained only to teach them the art of commanding. Carmel made them use their voices to make themselves heard from one hill to the other across the river, so that they should develop a good "word of command." At other times I would tell them what books say about tactics and strategy. They drew topographic maps and organized maneuvers. They received not only a non-commissioned officer's training, but even that of a cadet. A small "commission" of Hebraists worked out a Hebrew terminology for the exercises and commands which was later adopted for our battalion of Palestine volunteers and later still, in a dark hour, for the self-defense in Jerusalem. They were good-natured, intelligent, clean, brave young men. Many of them are living in Palestine today; for the others their grateful people Israel has not found a niche in Old-newland. I found two of them in New York after the war: Frug, a barber, and Kretschmar, a businessman. Several lie buried under a Magen David on the Mount of Olives.

It was already known in Whitechapel that the Legion was coming. At a meeting of the Zionist Committee, Sokolov himself expressed his change of mind and said to the younger members, "Don khaki now, so that later you may be able to don 'blue-white.'" Several hundred friends gathered around Harry First and awaited with impatience the day on which they could sign on; others murmured in the restaurants – "for" or "against." And in addition it was learned that the government was negotiating with St. Petersburg with a view to organizing conscription for aliens.

This was true. In Whitechapel, whisperings were heard that this had been "managed" by the Legionists. Jews hate to believe in history, a featureless power which creates facts whether we like them or not. Jews always seek a guilty human. Conscription had to come even if we had taken the trouble of disturbing the process. But I say quite frankly that I did not desire to disturb it in the least. On the contrary.

One day I received a telegram from Nabokov. "Take leave and come. Urgent."

At the embassy in Chatham Square he showed me a message from the Russian foreign minister, Terestshenko, asking the opinion of the ambassador on the question of conscription for Russian citizens in Britain. The British Government desired it. What was public opinion, British and Jewish, on the matter?

"Among Englishmen, Gentiles and Jews, there are no two opinions; all agree on conscription. Among the foreign Jews there are two opinions. One is that of the majority in Whitechapel – no. The other is that of my friends and myself – yes."

"What are your reasons?"

"First, because I am Continental, and consider the British system of a volunteer army to be one of Britain's greatest ineptitudes. I am heart and soul for conscription. As long as we have wars, participation in a war is a duty and not a sport for amateurs. Second, in the third year of war, it would be difficult for Garibaldi himself to find a sufficiently large number of volunteers. Enthusiasm has been quenched. Britain must also institute conscription. It is foolish to expect Whitechapel suddenly to display a desire for war in 1916, when the ordinary Britisher already lost such a desire in 1915; and it will be foolish and unjust to blame Whitechapel if it does not display that desire. But the fact remains that Whitechapel will be blamed, and among the British masses there will awaken a hatred the like of which has not yet been seen. This must be avoided. Conscription by all means!"

Nabokov assured me that he would reply to his minister in this spirit.

This is still my opinion today. War and military service are both abnormal things; I am one of those optimists who believe firmly that some day there will remain no trace of either. But as long as they exist, the volunteer system is the greatest injustice imaginable. Only the best patriots suffer on account of it; the indifferent ones remain at home – thus creating a premium on indifference. And it is not at all true that a volunteer army is more "heroic." The French soldiers at Verdun were all the products of conscription. Garibaldi once said that on the second day of service no difference remains between a volunteer and a conscript. And it is perfectly true. Every volunteer at some time regrets his step – but then he tells himself, "It is too late – I must remain a soldier." Which means that he has become a conscript. And every average conscript tells himself, "It's bad, but if

I am forced to be a soldier, I may as well be a thorough soldier." At that moment he becomes a volunteer.

In our battalions we had both volunteers and conscripts. Even in England several hundred signed on before they were called. The Palestine volunteers, the Argentinians, the Turkish prisoners – constituting together more than one third of the Legion – even had to battle with the government, particularly with Allenby's General Staff, before they were allowed to serve. But no difference ever made itself manifest. "Tailors" – as they called the Whitechapel recruits – ultimately became an honorable description, a synonym for first-class soldiers; and the "boys" of Whitechapel richly deserved it.

In the month of August there appeared, one after the other, two official announcements: conscription for Russian citizens in England, and the establishment of the Jewish Regiment. We were apportioned three rooms in the "recruiting department." I took my leave of Colonel Pownall, thanked him for his patience, tact and assistance, and transferred myself to London with three of our soldiers as officials. General Geddes informed me that Colonel Patterson had been ordered to hand over his Dublin Battalion to another commander and that he would arrive in London within a few days.

Before Patterson arrived, General Geddes called together a council of officers in his department, for the purpose of discussing the methods of our recruiting campaign. It was decided that apart from the general recruiting, an energetic propaganda campaign should be conducted in order to expound to the Jewish community both the moral and the Jewish national value of the Legion.

At the end of the meeting one of the officers remarked: "But we must take into account the inevitability of a strong counter-agitation. It's the same crowd that spoiled your first campaign last year, Sergeant J. I have received long reports: they're already going about spreading all kinds of false rumors."

I had already heard about this. My Whitechapel friends had prepared reports for me. The same people, perhaps in greater numbers, were again going about among the Whitechapel boys, telling them not to trouble themselves about any "conscription"; that Kerensky's government already regretted having consented; that the "Soviet of Workers' Deputies" would soon force it to rescind its decision; and that the best method was again to cause trouble and to refuse any service. But if they were to serve, then definitely not in the Jewish Regiment, for this was just a "trap"; they would not be sent to Palestine but to the worst and most dangerous of all fronts – to Flanders. And they needed no further proof of this than the fact that Lloyd George had told somebody, "We'll use Jews to fill up gas-holes," and Derby had said something else and a third had said this, that and the other.

But the officer in the recruiting department had still more explicit information.

"Have you heard of a certain Mr. Chicherin? He is not a Jew, but according to my information he is the real hidden wire puller."

Of Mr. Chicherin's role I, as the reader is aware, had already known for a long time. At that time I did not consider him to be a "wire puller"; just then he was more concerned with purely Russian affairs. But in his spare time, during those hours which one can devote to a hobby, to "trifles," he showed us the kindness of adding fuel to the Jewish flames. He was the source of the "assurances" that the St. Petersburg Soviet "would not permit." And why should he not be? Neither he nor his people would pay the price of our destruction. Zion or Dispersion, British friendship or antisemitism – to him it made no difference. His father was pro-Jewish, but his grandfather, the squire, had probably amused himself occasionally by stirring up trouble between his village Jews and the peasants, and watching to see what the end would be.

"I know about Mr. Chicherin," I replied, "but my friends and I have no longer any fear of this crowd. We shall print appeals, we shall arrange meetings, and our truth will drive away their lies. And I can assure you that this time the meetings will come off without any disturbance. We don't even need police. I have my men from Platoon Sixteen."

"H'm," replied the officer. "We are not so sanguine. We don't like this Mr. Chicherin, who is so keen on looking after the Jewish people."

Our meetings were not disturbed. Sergeant Ephraim Blitstein, of Alexandria, brought along a score of our strongest "mule drivers," Georgian "*shvilis*," burly boys from Odessa and Kiev, husky football players from the Jaffa gymnasium, Volga boys – and there was peace.

Mr. Chicherin's friends delivered fiery speeches at the meetings, attacking Zionism and militarism. We replied quietly but firmly. Freedom of speech – yes; freedom of noise – no.

Mr. Joseph King, in the conversation we had had in the National Liberal Club, had truly cast a prophetic evil eye at Mr. Chicherin. His prediction was fulfilled: his fate, however, was not prison, but a British internment camp.

As solace for his supporters, I can assure them that he probably had a much more comfortable and satisfying time there than his countrymen were destined to have in the "Cheka."

Chapter VIII
Meanders of State Wisdom

I must now relate an episode which in itself perhaps does not merit relating; namely, the strenuous efforts made by the assimilationists to destroy the Legion in embryo.

It would be enough to say briefly that they did not succeed. That the episode was characteristic of "Englishmen of the Jewish faith" is not sufficient reason to write about it – for we know that type in any case. But this episode was also characteristic of the British administrative machinery. That is why it is important, for we know far too little about this machinery. We Jews still believe in the legend that Britain is governed according to a preconceived plan; that in every matter the government lays down a definite line which is then followed out exactly and in a statesmanlike way. It is not so. Often, too often, their work presents an accurate picture of what the Germans used to call "*Russische Wirtschaft*" ("Russian business"): a decision is taken in one room, while it is being vitiated in practice in another. Ultimately there is always a compromise and a settlement, for the people itself is level-headed and cool; but any other people with such leaders would find itself in a fine pickle at least once a month. A famous example was provided in 1922, when the Wahabites declared war on King Hussein of Mecca. It was officially revealed in the House of Commons that the government had, at one and the same time, supported both the Wahabites and King Hussein with arms and ammunition: the item of expenditure was clearly set out in both the British and Indian budgets – but nobody had noticed it before. And these methods were manifest in matters small as well as big. For example, in this "démarche" of the assimilationists.

Patterson honestly sought a rapprochement with them, desiring agreement on their part to assist in making the Legion an honor and not a disgrace for all Jews. Immediately on his arrival in London he called a meeting, which was attended by Lionel de Rothschild, Edmund Sebag-Montefiore and others of our opponents; Dr. Weizmann, Major Amery and Major Ormsby-Gore were there from our side, together with another officer whose name we did not know. Lord Rothschild was there as well – later a good friend of the Regiment and chairman of the committee which assisted the soldiers, but at that time still a waverer. Patterson has described this meeting in his book, *With the Judeans in the Palestine Campaign.* I desire to add only a few words.

The majority of the meeting agreed that, whatever their opinions were, the Legion was an accomplished fact and it was the duty of everybody to make it successful. Captain Redcliffe Salaman, a M.O., and a member of one of the oldest Anglo-Jewish families, declared, "The Zionists have played us Columbus' egg-trick. They have confronted us with an accomplished fact and thus stopped all discussion. There is only one thing left for us – try to make the Regiment a success and a credit to the Jewish people." But Lionel de Rothschild and Sebag-Montefiore declared that they would not fall in, and that they would continue to fight. Immediately after the meeting they went to General Geddes and complained that "Patterson and his foreign sergeant were making Zionist propaganda in the same building as the recruiting department."

A few steps away from his department, at 10 Downing Street, the premier himself was preparing the ground in the War Cabinet for the Balfour Declaration; the same General Geddes himself had assisted me in ordering Magen Davids, Menoras, *Kadima* and blue-white insignia. But lack of system is a strong British tradition – and Geddes took fright and summoned Patterson to reprimand him.

There was an incident at that meeting which had a tragic ending. After the meeting Patterson showed me a scrap of paper on which was written in pencil, "I will come with you if you like. – N.P."

"Who is N.P.?" he asked. "This was given to me after Montefiore spoke; but I was so excited that I did not see by whom."

"Don't you know the handwriting or the initials?"

I also did not know. And in the trials and troubles of those days, the matter passed out of our minds.

Six weeks later we read that Captain Neil Primrose, a son of Lord Rosebery, had been killed on the Palestine front. His death made a deep impression on the Anglo-Jewish community, for the main branch of the Primrose family was half Jewish – descendants of Hannah Rothschild, who had married Lord Rosebery. It was known that the Primroses were very proud of their Jewish descent and that Neil Primrose especially had been eager to fight on the Palestine front.

Amery, on meeting Patterson at the war office, remarked, "Do you remember Neil Primrose? He was the officer I brought along to that meeting with your opponents. He was very interested in the Legion...."

If it had not been for a silly accident, he would have been with us in the Legion, and perhaps still alive today.

After that meeting the assimilationists formally declared war.

They sent a deputation to the war minister, Lord Derby. It consisted of Lord Swaythling, Major Lionel de Rothschild and others of that class from which it was afterward desired to recruit the second "fifty" for the Jewish Agency for Palestine. Their purpose was clear. It was a few months before the Balfour Declaration was to be issued; it was in the final step of their struggle against the Declaration, and they decided very logically that a Jewish Corps in Palestine would be far more "dangerous" from the anti-Zionist point of view than a mere paper promise.

They demanded of the minister that there should be no Jewish Regiment and that while foreign Jews should be enlisted, they should be distributed among the various battalions and on the different fronts – and not sent to Palestine.

Lord Derby, while refusing to dismember the regiment, agreed to deprive it of the name "Jewish," to treat it in the same way as all other regiments, and to send it wherever it might be required.

In half an hour we heard of this decision. Patterson, risking a court-martial, immediately sent a caustic letter to the adjutant-general. He wrote that he considered Derby's promise to the plutocrats a betrayal; that it meant that his recruits (of whom he already had several hundred at the new camp at Portsmouth) had been deceived; that he thought the decision scandalous and disgraceful, and that consequently he resigned his command there and then.

Dr. Weizmann and Mr. Amery went to Lord Milner, then also a member of the War Cabinet, and complained bitterly against Lord Derby's action. Milner, surprised and shocked, immediately saw Lord Derby, and half an hour later he returned with Lord Derby's agreement to meet a "counter-deputation" so that he should be in a position to effect a compromise. I reminded myself of my old article of faith: "The world's ruling caste are the journalists," and I proceeded to the office of the *Times* to see Mr. Steed. What I said was obvious; but I noted his replies verbatim.

"Tomorrow the *Times* will tell the War Office not to play the fool."

"But," I said, "Patterson doesn't want to stay, and I can't do without him."

"The *Times* will tell him to stay."

The next day Steed's editorial appeared. The War Office had not had such a drubbing throughout the war. The *Times* ridiculed their concerning themselves with a handful of plutocrats and forgetting the idealism of millions of Jews whose sympathies were worth something. If there was to be a compromise with the plutocrats, it was enough that the name should be changed; instead of "Jewish Regiment" let it be "Maccabean Regiment"; but its Jewish character must be strictly safeguarded, and it should be sent only to Palestine. "And we hope that Colonel Patterson, with whose indignation we can sympathize, will still change his decision."

After this editorial, as in the case of all other *Times* thunderbolts, the rest was but a simple formality. Lord Derby told the second deputation that the Legion would be purely Jewish, and that it would be sent to Palestine. But he thought that there was one aspect in which the gentlemen of the first deputation were not unjust: the honorable description, "Jewish," should not be applied to a new regiment which had not yet distinguished itself on the battlefield. Such a name had first to be earned; and he promised that when the Jewish soldiers had displayed their bravery in action, the Regiment would be granted both a Jewish name and a Jewish insignia. In the meantime we should have another honorable name – "Royal Fusiliers."

These promises, when the time came, he fulfilled. After the conquest, we were granted the description, "Judean Regiment," and the Menora with the Hebrew word, "*Kadima*." But from the very outset we did not lack "Jewishness." We had a Hebrew signboard outside our London recruiting depot. In the press and even in official documents we were always referred to as the "Jewish Regiment." At the front all our officers and men wore a Magen David on their sleeve, one battalion red, the second blue, and the third violet. Our padre was the Rev. M. Falk, an enthusiastic "Mizrahi," and himself a brave soldier under fire; and Colonel Patterson was compelled to learn all the laws and details of the *shohet*'s ritual, negotiating with the War Office and Portsmouth butchers about kosher meat, about veins and sinews and – I must stop, for while he knows the laws, I do not.

The "démarche" of the assimilationists had its results for me as well. One of them did me the special honor of protesting against my recruiting propaganda.

Beilin and Pinsky, who had collaborated in the *Tribune,* which Grossman had edited in the previous year's campaign, compiled a pamphlet on the purpose of the Jewish Legion. As the conscription regulations permitted a choice between serving here and serving in Russia, this pamphlet also showed that Russian military service was far from pleasant.

The pamphlet was published at the expense of the Recruiting Department. The Department supplied me with 35,000 addresses of aliens who had so far not enlisted (it is characteristic of the British system that among these names and addresses I found my own as well). They also supplied me with 35,000 envelopes, "On His Majesty's Service," and with ten officials to write the addresses.

The day after Lord Derby had met the assimilationist delegation, I received a telephoned order to be at the adjutant-general's office at eleven o'clock sharp. I went along. Patterson was already there. The adjutant-general, Sir Neville MacReady, was seated at the table, his face wearing an official expression. It looked like trouble.

"Do you recognize this?" he asked, and handed me a bulky English manuscript. I read through the first lines.

"The beginning is reminiscent, sir," I said, "of a Yiddish brochure which we have sent out. Badly translated."

"I am told that the Russian embassy is very annoyed," he declared. "This brochure is filled with attacks on the Russian Army."

"That means that the translation is worse than bad. There are no such attacks in our pamphlet. Secondly, I saw Mr. Nabokov, the Russian ambassador, both yesterday and today. The only matter we discussed was the Legion, but he did not even mention the brochure. You can ring him and ask him, sir."

His voice rose.

"Who gave you the right, sergeant, to distribute the brochure in official envelopes?"

I looked at him blankly (looking is not prohibited). His department gives me the addresses, which are a state secret; gives me 35,000 envelopes; gives me officials, and he, the master of the War Office, asks me how it can be? Heavens! What kind of system is this? Can any foreign N.C.O. occupy a room in Whitehall, give orders and instructions, perhaps even stop the war? It is fortunate for them that I am what some of my friends call a "militarist."

But Sir Neville MacReady possessed intelligence and a sense of humor. As I dared not laugh, he burst out himself and said to Patterson, "Send 'Sergeant J.' to your camp at Portsmouth. I hope that he'll show himself to be as good a soldier as he is a propagandist."

I saluted and went out. Ten minutes later Patterson appeared in the corridor.

"Sir," I asked, "when shall I leave for Portsmouth?"

"Not at all," replied the Irishman, who had had too much to do with man-eating lions to take a mere general seriously. "In my battalion I am master, and I want you to stay in London to do the recruiting. Come along to the depot and I'll give you an order."

I boarded a taxi and drove to see Nabokov.

"Did you protest against this brochure, Constantin Dimitrievitch?" I asked him.

"I have never in my life seen it or heard of it."

"Perhaps Sablin?"

E. A. Sablin, the secretary, was summoned. The same reply.

Nabokov wrote a formal note to this effect. Sablin affixed the embassy seal, they tied it up together with the brochure and sealed the tape. I took the package to Amery, and he sent it on to the adjutant-general with a letter I did not read but whose contents I could well imagine.

MacReady is not an English name. I have a suspicion that Sir Neville is himself an Irishman, for he treated the matter in true "sporting" fashion – by forgetting it. He knew that I remained in London, giving interviews and delivering lectures – he even mentioned it in his letters to Patterson – but made no protest whatever. And he remained a friend of the Legion. He thrust Patterson's caustic letter in his pocket and simply said, "Don't worry; it'll be all right."

Who it was who gave him the false information that the embassy was annoyed I do not know. But it is interesting that this incident took place at the same time as the deputation of the assimilationists saw Lord Derby. And in certain quarters there existed no scruples about a little "informing." I later saw through the whole thing quite clearly. I shall yet tell about it.

They continued their attempts at putting spokes in our wheel, The adjutant-general was permitting Jews of other regiments, even at the front, to apply for transfers to our Regiment. Many of them were eager to do so, and the stiffening they would have provided to our men would have been most useful. Suddenly, however, all the Army rabbis in France began to preach that it was a shameful act for Jews to serve in our regiment. We heard that even the chief chaplain, Reverend Michael Adler himself, took this text for his sermons. Whether this was true or not, I do not know, but all the Jewish chaplains were under his charge; and that he issued the instructions, I have, I regret, no doubts. Thus, instead of thousands of transfers, there were only several hundred.

Mrs. Weizmann was of great service. Together with Mrs. Patterson, she created the "Jewish Regiment Care and Comforts Committee," in which the wives of nearly all the leading Zionists took part: Mrs. Joseph Cowen, Mrs. Eder, Mrs. Paul Goodman, Mrs. Charles Rothschild, the late Nina Davis-Salaman, the gifted poetess, Miss Greenberg (the daughter of the editor of the *Jewish Chronicle*), Mrs. Arshavsky (the wife of the engineer), and many others, to all of whom I extend my thanks. They all used to spend days and even nights at our depot, cooking and washing for the recruits. At first Major Knowles – a friend of Patterson – was in charge of the depot; later a Jew, Major Schonfield, who had been a friend from the beginning; and both proved untiring in their efforts.

My office was also in the depot. I had to write letters to the United States, Canada, Argentina, Russia, neutral countries, wherever Jewish young men were to be found. In the main, this correspondence bore no fruit whatever. Cast your bread upon the waters.... From the United States, Canada and Argentina, soldiers *did* come, but I doubt whether this was the result of the work of our little office. The Legion was making propaganda for itself; the role of its creators had ended.

One occurrence only gave me satisfaction in those days. I found Margolin. He had been wounded and brought to a London hospital, where I visited him. I knew his story well, from his brother in St. Petersburg – the editor of Efron's Russian and Jewish Encyclopaedias – and still more from the legends I had heard about him in Palestine. His family had emigrated to Palestine in the first days of the "Bilu," when Eliezer was still a child. They settled at Rehovot. Eliezer distinguished himself as a colonist and as a marksman and horseman. "He sits his horse like a Bedouin and shoots like an Englishman," the Arabs used to say of him. With the crisis in the early nineties, he went to Australia, wandered about, worked in the bush, plowed, dug, until he settled in a city and became a businessman, at the same time joining the Australian Territorial Army. When the war broke out he was a lieutenant and was one of the first volunteers for the front. He served for a long time in Egypt and was promoted by stages to the post of "second-in-command" of his battalion in Flanders. He was a huge, strong, silent man, every inch a soldier, a father and brother to his boys, with a masterly ability for organizing, and with an eye for every detail in his battalion, from blankets and grease to kitchen utensils.

"Come to us, Lazar Markovitch," I said to him.

"I am afraid."

"Afraid?"

"I am afraid of Jews. One has to talk too much."

But he came. The adjutant-general assisted in having him transferred from the Australian Army to the British, and Eliezer Margolin became the colonel of our second battalion – the "Thirty-ninth Royal Fusiliers."

I cannot write of the life of our soldiers at Portsmouth. I only visited the camp once for a few days and felt like a complete stranger. Colonel Patterson introduced me to the few officers in his room. He could not invite me to the Officers' Mess. In the Sergeants' Mess I found some of my old friends and a few of my comrades from Platoon Sixteen. But the other sergeants were somewhat shy – and so was I.

Late at night, I remember, I stood alone in the snow in the middle of the moonlit camp and, watching, lost myself in thought. Low barracks on all sides, in each of them hundreds of young men – the Jewish Legion... a dream. So long dreamed, so hardly achieved, and not mine, not built by me, not brought up by me. Just like the story of Aladdin's palace built by spirits. Who is Aladdin? What is Aladdin? Nothing. An accident presented him with an old rusty lamp and when he wanted to clean it and began rubbing it with a rag, the genie suddenly appeared and built him a palace. The palace stands, and will remain standing, but nobody any longer needs either Aladdin or his lamp. I wondered. Perhaps we are all Aladdins. Each of our thoughts is a magic lamp which has the power to call up creative spirits. You must only never tire of "rubbing." Rub, rub and rub again – until you become superfluous. Perhaps every true creation consists in the creator's becoming superfluous.

Thenceforth I became superfluous. And I am glad that my story has reached the stage where I can stop using the word "I" so frequently.

It is not my fault that in telling of the birth-pangs of the Jewish Legion I have had to use the word at every step. At meetings in America the worthy chairman used to introduce me as the "leader of the Jewish Legion." That I never was, and could not be. The Legion in Palestine consisted of three battalions, all together about five thousand men, led by three colonels with much military experience. In one of these battalions, I was one of about twenty lieutenants, commander of a platoon of fifty or sixty men. For I was promoted, two days before our departure for Palestine, to the rank of lieutenant; and even this had come about with difficulty, for according to the British constitution no foreigner may be an officer in the Army. Patterson used to say, laughingly, "There are only two exceptions, the Kaiser and you – and he's out." I do not know whether this was correct, but I had just as little say in the Legion as the Kaiser had in the British Army. I had no objections to this position; it was just as it should be. I tried to be a good lieutenant, just as I had tried to wash the tables successfully in the Sergeants' Mess at Winchester; and I delight in both memories.

On the second of February, 1918, the first Jewish Battalion, with shining bayonets, marched through the City of London and Whitechapel. The soldiers had been brought from Portsmouth to London two days earlier and treated with an abundance of celebration. They slept in the Tower of London, among the monuments of six centuries of English history. The shining bayonets were also an exception: the citizens of London had fought for generations for the privilege of not allowing the King's soldiers to carry their bayonets in the City – but they permitted us to carry ours. At the entrance to the Mansion House stood the lord mayor, dressed in his mayoral robes, and took the salute from the Jewish soldiers. Next to him stood Major R—, one of our bitterest opponents – looking important and proud, taking a delight in something which he had only narrowly failed to destroy.

From the City the battalion marched to Whitechapel. There the adjutant-general – the same Sir Neville MacReady – was awaiting us with his staff. There were tens of thousands of Jews in the streets, at the windows and on the roofs. Blue-white flags were over every shop door; women crying with joy, old Jews with fluttering beards murmuring "*Shehecheyanu*"; Patterson on his horse, laughing and bowing, and wearing a rose which a girl had thrown him from a balcony; and the boys, those "tailors," shoulder to shoulder, their bayonets dead level, each step like a single clap of thunder, clean, proud, drunk with the national anthem, with the noise of the crowds, and with the sense of a holy mission, unexampled since the day when Bar Kokhba, in Betar, not knowing whether there would ever be others to follow and take up the struggle, threw himself upon his sword.

Long life to you, my "tailors" of Whitechapel and Soho, Leeds and Manchester! You were good tailors: you found the torn rags of Jewish honor in the street and you sewed them together – to make a beautiful, whole and everlasting flag.

Chapter IX
Training Camp and G.H.Q.

Two days later we left Southampton for France – Egypt – Palestine.

It took us ten days to traverse France and Italy. But they were not difficult days. One inevitably gained the impression that both France and Italy had been created for the express purpose of insuring the comfort of English soldiers. At each station, from Cherbourg to Taranto, we found an English R.T.O. who seemed to be the real proprietor of the railway.

Every two days we stopped for a day and a night at a rest camp, where there were English doctors, nurses and orderlies. They were like villages of barracks and tents, with large marquees for the men, the sergeants and the officers, a chemist, a hospital, a concert hall, even a *kalabush* – the name given by our Zion Mule Corps boys, under Egyptian influence, to the military prison. Our battalion possessed a first-class concert orchestra of real music-hall artists; it was admitted on all sides that they were probably the best of all those that had honored the camps with a recital. It must be added that their repertoire contained nothing even remotely Jewish – except for "*Hatikva*" which, at Colonel Patterson's orders, concluded every concert.

The men were gloriously happy. I remember one day when we were slowly passing through the French Riviera – Nice, Monaco, sparkling in the full bloom of spring. Never in their lives had our Whitechapel boys imagined that such beauty existed, and from every window of fifty carriages there burst a spontaneous exclamation of joy.

Of our thirty officers, twenty were Jews – transfers from other regiments. Most of them had at that time heard very little about Zionism; the Officers' Mess, after meals, often had the appearance of a discussion-evening of the good old days in Minsk or Kishinev. Are the Jews a nation? What is nationality? Can one be a Zionist and a British patriot at the same time? They often tried to drag me into the discussion – but I had long forgotten how one "proves" such problems.

I left this honor to younger Zionist "recruits." Horace Samuel, a not unknown writer (later he became an important barrister in Jerusalem, and in his fantastic novel, *Quisto box*, one may find a good humorous description of Palestine after the war), used to take hold of the coat-button of the long-nosed Harris, who stubbornly defended assimilation, and show him, in his Oxford accent and with many philosophical and classical allusions, that "nationality is just an inward attitude"; and to press his point Samuel would call up the adjutant, Liddle, a typically cold Englishman of the public-schoolboy type, and ask: "Come on, Harris, will you tell me that you and he are of the same nationality?"

The padre, Reverend Mr. Falk, held out bravely against the general attack of a whole regiment of skeptical lieutenants, who pleaded that being a Zionist had nothing to do with eating kosher food. He stood like a rock by his principle. "It isn't a question of eating. It is the principle that the Jew must always fight against all temptation, control and discipline himself at every step, and build a Zion of purity in his heart before building a Zion for his people."

Captain Davis, the M.O. (Redcliffe Salaman had remained at Portsmouth with Colonel Margolin), would complain laughingly, "I am suddenly ordered to remind myself that I am a Jew and to join the Jewish Legion! That means that henceforth I am a conscripted Zionist. Well, I'll play the game."

And he wrote a song for the men, permeated with nationalism and enthusiasm, for the difference between a volunteer and a conscript is not, after all, so great.

The best Zionist was the colonel. His alignments were convincing.... Gideon, Deborah, King David, Migdal, the moon in the valley of Ayalon.... The padre tried to prove that Patterson was not even a General Zionist but a Mizrahist. And it is a fact that the colonel saw to it – how, I do not know – that every Saturday should find us in a rest camp; in the morning we would have synagogue parade, with all the officers and men, even Christians, standing with their hats on, with the Zionist flag flying from a tall flagpole, with the Scroll of the Law given to us by the Portsmouth community, and with the concert choir singing all the prayers and "*Hatikva*" and the English anthem at the end. The Reverend Mr. Falk would deliver a sermon, with consistent brilliance, for the young rabbi was highly educated, learned in the voluminous Jewish traditional literature, and had an outstanding knowledge of history. He drew freely on the party rivalry of the Pharisees and the Sadducees for his analogies, was a strong admirer of the Essenes, bitterly attacked the Hellenists, energetically praised the Zealots, and attacked the theories of Wellhausen and his pupil, Dr. Benzion Mossinsohn of the Tel Aviv Gymnasium.... The Jews of Sydney are to be congratulated on their present rabbi.

We did not stop at any of the big towns and saw no Jews. Only once, in Italy – I think it was in Rimini – when we were marching with our flag to the railway station, an old man suddenly rushed out from a gate and, pointing at himself, shouted: "Yehudi! Yisrael! Eviva!"

In Taranto, our final rest camp, where we had to kick our heels for a week waiting for the convoy of Japanese destroyers, Patterson and Falk went to a cabinetmaker in the town and ordered an ark of the finest wood. At the Sabbath parade, the Scroll was placed in this ark with much ceremony, and the colonel said to the men, in all seriousness: "With this talisman on board, we need have no fear of German submarines."

The voyage occupied less than two days. It was peaceful and quiet; we had no seasickness, though Sergeant Shifrin, the chief wit of the battalion, would conduct a daily sick parade, in conformity with regulation. The men were ordered into a row on the deck and Shifrin rapidly fired his commands: "Right dress!... Number!... Two paces forward march!... Head forward bend!... As you were!..."

The Sephardic community in Alexandria gave us a rousing welcome. Again I found our old friends of the "Gabbari" days: Chief Rabbi Raphael della Pergola, Baron and Baroness de Menasseh, Edgar Suares and Joseph de Picciotto. "The Zion Mule Corps was our son, the Jewish Legion is our grandson," they said. In the main synagogue they arranged an impressive service, attended by the governor, generals, Allied and neutral consuls and Arab notables.

The same happened in Cairo. General Allenby had already set up his headquarters in Palestine not far from Be'er Yaakov, but the English High Commissioner, Sir Reginald Wyndham, took the salute of the marching battalion before the gate of the Residency and listened to the "*Hatikva*" at the salute.... Far away still were those gloomy days of 1919 when General Money, the military governor of Palestine, in the presence of important Jewish, English and Arab personalities, remained seated when "*Hatikva*" was played!

We were encamped at Helmieh, a village near Cairo, where the battalion was to complete its training. It was burning hot and drill was possible only until 9 A.M. and after 5 P.M. Almost every week there was a ball – either in the town in honor of the battalion, or in camp in honor of the Cairo Jewish community.

In addition to my ordinary duties as a platoon commander, I was given another "job" at Helmieh.

According to military regulations, all letters written by the men must be scrutinized by an officer. Among the officers I was the only one who could read Hebrew and Yiddish. As a result, I was ordered to look through all the letters which were not written in English. It was then that I discovered that there were several Lithuanians in our battalion – Lithuanian Christians. They had previously worked in a coal mine somewhere near Glasgow, and when called up, they had asked to serve with us. I knew, of course, nothing about Lithuanian except that they called Germany "Voketja," and a Pole "Lenkas." It should have been my duty to "resign," but this would only have meant that their letters would be destroyed, for where, in Egypt of all places, could anybody be found who understood Lithuanian? I therefore decided to take the risk of the Allies being defeated and stamped "O.K." on their letters. But there was one thing which I did make out. These Lithuanians were about the only men who used to describe the journey, mention geographical names, discuss the particular purposes of the Legion – the only ones who did not concern themselves only with their private affairs. In their letters I continually came across such words as "Nice," "Italy," "Egypt," even "Jerusalem" and "Zionism."

In the hundreds of Jewish letters it was very seldom that one found such a thing. "The road is pretty," "The compartment is rather crowded," "Thank God, the sea was calm." But then there always came the main items: "How are the children?" "How are Hannah's teeth?" and "Joe's measles?" "Don't be lonely, dear. Have you installed the gas in the kitchen?" Here you found an indescribable love, not of a country, or of a town or a street, but of his home and his family. I often wonder whether this love is not better than patriotism. For is it not the true foundation of patriotism? Give these people a "home," not in a strange country where they are immigrants of yesterday, but a home where the house and the street and the town and the country are interwoven with one another, bricks in the same building, where you cannot break one without disturbing all – and you will perhaps have created the psychology of Bar Kokhba's Zealots.

Often I was almost ashamed to look so deep into the sanctum sanctorum of a stranger's soul. I made one rule for myself, however – never to look at the address on the envelope. I do not regret the hours I spent in reading those letters, for they showed me that the "tailor" has a home and knows how to live. I never found anything in them that needed censoring, though in several I found strong condemnations of the censor himself; but who it was that penned these condemnations I had no idea, for I carefully replaced the letters in the envelopes without looking at the address.

We were waiting for new arrivals. A few days before our departure from England we had received a telegram from New York, signed by Brainin, Ben-Zvi and Ben-Gurion, which informed us of the launching of the recruiting campaign for the Legion in America. The Greek government had announced that volunteer recruiting would be permitted in Salonika. A message came from Buenos Aires signed by Vladimir Herman: "English consent obtained." And a recruiting office had been opened in Egypt itself.

But the most encouraging news had come from Palestine. Hardly had the train entered the railway station at Cairo, when a khaki-clad young man ran up to me. "My name is Aloni," he said. "I have been sent from Tel Aviv to welcome the Legion on behalf of the Palestine volunteers."

And he told me of a great movement in that part of Palestine which had already been liberated – Jerusalem, Tel Aviv and Jaffa, and the colonies of Judea; and even in the north, which was still in the hands of the Turk – in Zikhron-Yaakov and Hadera, in Haifa, and in the colonies of Upper and Lower Galilee – there was great enthusiasm among the young people, some of whom had broken through the Turkish border patrols and had arrived at Petah Tikva asking, "Where is the Legion?"

One morning Patterson told me to pack: "I have been given permission to go to Palestine with you."

In the train neither of us slept the whole night long – not so much because of my excitement as because of the colonel's. It is difficult to describe what it means to a Protestant to "live through" such names as Sinai, Gaza, Palestine.

In his childhood he had sat by the fire for hours every Sunday,

Lieutenant Vladimir Jabotinsky

Captain Joseph Trumpeldor

Major James de Rothschild

Peter Rutenberg

Colonel John H. Patterson, D. S. O.

אלכסנדריה של מצרים, יום ח' אדר התרע"ה.

א) נוסד באלכסנדריה גדוד של מתנדבים עברים, אשר [illegible] את [illegible] ברשות ממשלת אנגליה [illegible] בכבוד להשתתף בשחרור ארץ-ישראל.

ב) בראש הגדוד יעמוד שלטון, הממונה מאת הועד המיסד, והמתנדבים יבחרו שלושה צירים להשתתף בשלטון.

ג) כל מתנדב יעבוד להקריב את כחו ואת חייו לשחרור ארץ-ישראל, ולהכנע לשלטון ולבלי לעזוב את הגדוד עד קץ פעולתו.

ד) כל מתנדב יקבל מאת הועד המיסד מזון ומעון. ~~[illegible]~~

~~[illegible]~~

[illegible] ז'בוטינסקי

[illegible] ז'בוטינסקי

יוסף טרומפלדור

[illegible], 35

[illegible] Rue Colon Pompe

N 67.

[illegible] 18 [illegible],

[illegible] 22 [illegible]

[illegible] 23

[illegible] 19 [illegible]

[illegible] Hotel Metropole [illegible]

[illegible] 21 [illegible]

[illegible] 18 [illegible]

[illegible] 23 Исаак Марьянавский

[illegible] 22 Hotel Metropole [illegible]

Hotel „Metropole" [illegible] 18 [illegible]

[illegible] 19 [illegible]

יוסף [illegible] 19 [illegible]

[illegible] 33 [illegible]

The Resolution to form the Jewish Legion

Leopold S. Amery

Engineer Isaac Arshevsky

Henry Wickham Steed

Colonel Eliezer Margolin

Field Marshal Viscount Allenby

Reverend M. Falk

The Jewish Regiment marching through the city of London

The Jewish Regiment marching in Plymouth

Ze'ev Gluskin

Meir Grossman

Vladimir Jabotinsky (in the second row, third from right) with a group of ranks in the Jewish Legion, Plymouth

The choir of the Jewish regiment

Vladimir Jabotinsky with some leaders of the *Hitnadvut*

A group of Palestine volunteers. (First row, extreme right: M. Arber)

Poster used in recruiting campaign in Palestine

A group of legionaries. Holding the rifle is sculptor Jacob Epstein

Bayonet drill. Epstein is from right

Colonel Patterson in Transjordan

American legionaries at the Western Wall, Jerusalem

Welcoming ceremony for the Legion at the Great Synagogue of Alexandria

The 39th Battalion R. F. camped on Mt. Scopus, outside Jerusalem

Nurses volunteering for Jewish Legion

A group of Palestine volunteers

A group of American recruits in the 40th Battalion. Holding the flag: Israel Rosenberg.

The 38th Battalion in the Jordan Valley.

Colonel Patterson in Palestine

Vladimir Jabotinsky (fourth from right) with members of Betar
at the temporary grave of Trumpeldor his comrades at Tel Hai

Trumpeldor Monument in Tel Hai

quietly listening to his father reading chapters of the Bible. Suez Canal! To me it was something great, a tremendous engineering feat. But to Colonel Patterson it was a personal memory, bringing back to him a picture of his old home, and the beautiful Bible stories, which he had heard even before being told the first legends about the Irish mountain spirits and witches of Queen Deirdre, for whose sake so many heroes gave up their lives. For him it meant the crossing of the Red Sea, Moses with his patriarchal beard, Pharaoh's iron chariots, pillars of fire and smoke.

We saw the moon give way to the rose hues of dawn; then the sun came. Around us was always the desert, here and there relieved by tufts of grass. Then a little green: Gaza – to me a gray, dusty and dry Arab village, to my colonel a memory of Samson and merry-making Philistines. Then desert again. And suddenly a new world, a green eucalyptus wood followed by vineyards, white houses with red roofs in the distance – another world, a piece of Europe.

I heard the colonel ask the inspector, a soldier, "What place is this?"

"Doyran."

Here I had a taste for the first time of that attitude to Jewish work which had become a tradition with Allenby's staff. "Doyran?" It was our colony, Rehovot. Doyran is the name of an Arab village not even mentioned on the map. But Allenby had instituted this tradition. To him "Petah Tikva" was "Mulebis," "Be'er Yaakov" was "Bir-Salem." The only exception to the rule was Rishon-le-Zion, which was called "Rishon" – for Rishon wine was very popular and it would have been sacrilege to give a bottle of cognac a name taken from a people so prohibitionist as the Moslem Arabs.

We alighted at Be'er Yaakov. Not far from the colony, surrounding two large houses previously owned by a German farmer, were a number of tents and barracks – G.H.Q., General Allenby's headquarters. Here we separated. The colonel went to meet the commander-in-chief, and I was taken to Tel Aviv. In the evening we exchanged impressions. Mine were pleasant; his were not. For I had visited the bride, a poor bride awaiting the coming of the bridegroom, believing devoutly all the while that he loved her; Patterson had visited the bridegroom's rich father.

I had found Jaffa and Tel Aviv in a state of unbounded enthusiasm. I say Jaffa and Tel Aviv. Today one hardly mentions Jaffa. Then Tel Aviv was a town of three thousand inhabitants, and not really a town but a few score houses surrounding the Gymnasium – a clean, Westernized suburb for intellectuals. Most of the Jews lived in two parts of Jaffa: Neve Shalom and Neve Tzedek.

Approaching the town I met a ten-year-old boy whom I took with me, as he had promised to show me the way to my old friends, Eliahu Berlin and Bezalel Jaffe. He told me the latest news: forty thousand Jewish soldiers were coming in English ships; at the head of this army was General James Rothschild, the Baron's son. I had not the heart to tell him that so far we were but one battalion. But I had to tell my friends in Tel Aviv, and though their expectations were not so great as those of the boy, I felt that they were disappointed.

But their enthusiasm was created by something which completely overshadowed even our Legion – their own volunteer Legion. Its initiator and leader was Moses Smilansky, a man of over forty, a well-known Hebrew writer (*Hawaja Musa*) and one of the most highly respected colonists in Rehovot. He was immediately sent for, and he came with a group of workers from the colony – all volunteers. In Jaffa and Tel Aviv, too, all the volunteers were workers, or college graduates who were preparing to join the workers' movement. Berl Katznelson, later editor of *Davar*, Yavnieli, who years ago first brought Yemenites to Palestine, Dov Hos, Eliahu Golomb and many others today prominent in the Labor Movement, were the leading spirits among the volunteers. Only Hapoel Hatzair (Young Workers Movement) was adopting an attitude of aloofness toward the Movement, and even among them there was a division of opinion – one of the leaders, Swerdlow, and a number of other members having enlisted.

"Enlisted," that is to say, in their own organization, for the government had not yet given its consent. They had handed in a petition, signed by several hundred, in January, but had received no reply.

Yet they were certain that with our coming their petition would be granted.

"How many are you?" I asked.

"Nearly fifteen hundred. One-third are girls who want to serve as a Red Magen David group, though many of them hope that the English will agree to create a regiment of Amazons."

In the grounds of the girls' school they arranged an improvised parade of the Jaffa volunteers. Dov Hos, who had been an officer in the Turkish Army, was the instructor. One glance was sufficient to show what excellent material we had here – slim, alert, with impatient eyes; though sunken cheeks testified to the years of hunger under Turkey. These were the tidings I brought to Colonel Patterson. His story was of an altogether different kind.

General Allenby had exhibited much coldness toward both the London regiment and the Palestine volunteers. He had inherited from Kitchener a strong antagonism to "fancy regiments." Exactly what he said about Jewish soldiers I do not know – Patterson refrained from telling it to me and he says nothing about it in his book. But he emphasized one thing: It was not Allenby himself who was the chief opponent, but his chief of staff, a certain general Louis Bols, who two years later did nothing to prevent the Jerusalem pogrom. Unhappily silent, we paced to and fro on the dusty road among the cactus bushes. Looking back on those days one can see how they provided prophetic introduction to the Military Administration. On the one side, enthusiasm, hope, preparedness for any sacrifice, impatience to fight and to create; on the other, cold, skeptical eyes and a strange reproachful attitude, opposed to everything unusual, to everything not banal, not routine – against everything tinged with "fancy" – like Zionism.

But the colonel was not one of those who remain depressed for long. He soon shook off his frown.

"It doesn't matter," he said. "We have had greater difficulties before this. It will be all right. I am certain that the commander-in-chief will still change his mind."

There was truth in what Patterson said, even too much truth. For not once but ten times did Allenby change his mind, about both the Legion and the whole Zionist question.

Several weeks afterward he gave his consent to recruiting in Palestine, then again delayed the matter for months; then promised to create a Jewish Brigade with Patterson as general, then withdrew his promise, though it was contained in black and white in a letter.

It is a remarkable but notorious fact that the strongest of soldiers are often weak and influenced with the utmost ease. As a general, Allenby was a good strategist – at any rate, they say so and I am not qualified to judge. But they found it necessary to make him a statesman as well. And here he showed himself strong only as an "executive" – only as the executor of the counsel of others, and not as the true moving spirit; a big "motor-car" which can be driven by anybody with a little skill and a little luck. This combination is always a dangerous one. A man who, because of his career and outlook, had gained an established reputation for power and a strong will (Allenby's subordinates at G.H.Q. called him the "Bull of Bashan"), deep down in his heart, did not know what to do and must of necessity seek counselors. This is a very dangerous combination: usually only those people who suit themselves to the "Bull of Bashan" legend can influence him, for they help him to appear just as terrible as his reputation makes out, and always counsel him against "sentimentalism" and "softness." Allenby hardly seemed to be anti-Jewish and was probably not even anti-Zionist – he was scarcely the type of man to have any theoretical attitudes at all; but simply because of his tendency to heed such counselors, to regret any action which seemed to imply a concession to "idealistic humbug," he created in his staff and in his army a poisoned antisemitic atmosphere, the like of which I cannot recollect in Czarist Russia or anywhere else. His government, of course, had a different opinion of Allenby as a statesman, and went on entrusting him with important functions (Egypt after the War!), which, in my humble judgment, he mismanaged. Years later, I asked an Englishman who had lived for many years in foreign parts and who could therefore better judge his countrymen, "How is it? Don't they know that he is not suited to the role?"

He replied, "The English people always like a man to be big, handsome and not too bright."

Chapter x

The Joy of Hebrew Palestine

Immediately on our return to Helmieh, Colonel Patterson formed a "recruiting squad" for Palestine, consisting of officers with a knowledge of Hebrew; at the head of the group he placed Lieutenant Lipsey, with the order: "In one month you must be speaking Hebrew like Isaiah himself."

He laughingly added that he had himself learned "Hebrew" in Gallipoli. And indeed, the men of the Zion Mule Corps would often quote some of the gems which fell from his lips, like "*lishtot et hasusim*" ("to drink the horses"). But Lipsey's knowledge was sufficient – he was a member of an Orthodox Glasgow family and knew his prayer-book.

"Quite enough," said the padre. "All that you need can be found in the Eighteen Benedictions."

Lipsey, however, also taught the men the Hebrew command terminology, which had been compiled in Platoon Sixteen, and his recruiting squad began its work with gusto. The colonel considered it not a moment too soon: he was convinced that with the Lord of

Hosts, General Allenby's opinion was of just as little importance as that of Lord Kitchener.

And he was right. Shortly before Passover, the second Jewish battalion, commanded by Colonel Margolin and consisting more than half of Americans, arrived. Shortly afterward the "Zionist Commission" came, with Dr. Weizmann at its head and with Captain Ormsby-Gore as official intermediary between the Commission and G.H.Q. Major James Rothschild was also a member of the Commission and at the same time an officer in Margolin's battalion. General Allenby had to admit that Whitehall had set its face firmly toward Zionism and a Legion and that there was no help for it.

But for a long time the volunteer movement remained "unpopular" and even "dangerous." Friends of the G.H.Q. tendered the Zionist Commission some "careful" advice – to "steer clear" of the volunteers. And we love "careful" advice: we like to consider it "statesman-like," even when by so acting we harm important and useful work.

There was a dreadful moment when I feared that this "carefulness" would really hinder the volunteer movement. Smilansky had called together a mass meeting of all the volunteers in Rehovot. Nearly a thousand came from Jerusalem, the majority on foot, for traveling by train meant procuring a military permit, and they had no money for wagons – wagons, for there was no such thing as motor transport in Palestine. So they came on foot, which meant two days in the burning sun.

The Volunteers' Committee invited all the members of the Zionist Commission; not one of them came. I was at my wits' end. Patterson would not have been afraid to appear at the meeting, though Rehovot was only a stone's throw from G.H.Q. and from the irate General Bols, but Patterson was in Egypt. In despair I hurried to G.H.Q. to General Clayton (later he was civil secretary in Herbert Samuel's administration) and asked him to send an officer or at least a few written words of encouragement.

"I can't do it. Tell them that they are brave young men and that I hope…"

This was all I could carry with me to the meeting at Rehovot. But I found that I was mistaken in them: they had no need of encouragement. Their own enthusiasm and confidence were enough. With thundering applause they again proclaimed their will to fight for Palestine. They went so far as to decide to march immediately to Be'er Yaakov to demand an audience of General Allenby. I just managed to dissuade them. It was very "careful" of me – and to this day I regret it. I am convinced that it would have brought the recruiting campaign several months nearer.

Yet that meeting did not fail to have its effect on Headquarters. Near the building where it took place was the tent of an officer – a captain whose name I did not know. After the meeting he called me in.

"What is this?"

"Jewish volunteers. General Clayton gave me a message for them."

"Curious people," he said, "pushing themselves into the army, healthy and strong, when nobody compels them to. Who ever heard of such a thing – in the fourth year of war, too! And so many! I saw them marching – there seemed to be no end of them. How many were there? Three thousand?"

"H'm," I answered "carefully." "I didn't count, but a good many."

"Fine fellows," he said, "and they can march. I must send in a report." So they did "come" to Headquarters after all, though only on paper.

Of the volunteer movement – which released a wave of enthusiasm the like of which even its opponents admit was not seen either before or afterward – I unfortunately saw very little. At the beginning of June my battalion was already at the front, in the Mountains of Ephraim between Jerusalem and Shechem. For three days I was in Jerusalem delivering addresses – which were quite superfluous – and there I saw just a little of this unforgettable phenomenon. I was approached by old mothers, young mothers, Sephardim and Ashkenazim, who complained that the doctors had "shamed" their sons – by not accepting them for service. "I daren't show myself in the street for shame," was their plaint. A sickly Jew, who looked like Methuselah's grandfather, came to protest that he had not been able to deceive the doctor: he had said that he was forty, but the doctor was most unkind.... As for the youngsters, there was nothing that could stop them. Yet I heard that what I saw in Jerusalem was as nothing compared to the excitement which raged in Jaffa and among the workers in the colonies.

Major Rothschild, the leader of the recruiting campaign, asked me to visit Jaffa before returning to my battalion. At the meeting there I saw all my friends of the meeting at Rehovot: Smilansky, Hos, Golomb, Berl Katznelson with his Poale Zionists, Swerdlow with his Zeire-Zion minority, Yavnieli with his Yemenites, young Beilis, the son of Mendel Beilis, Uziel, the son of the Sephardic rabbi of Jaffa, with a fine group of Sephardim... And among them the recruiting party, many old friends who had endured the black and bitter years of loneliness and disillusionment – Arshavsky, now a corporal, Harry First, a private, and the oldest, the first of them all, the Gabbari and Zion Mule Corps men – Sergeant Nissel Rosenberg, the converts from the Volga, the Georgian "*shvilis*," and everywhere, on the galleries roundabout, a mass of Jaffa citizens, men, women and children, dressed in their poor Sabbath best; girls with flowers in their hair or carrying Zionist flags; English officers, Italian officers of a detachment stationed at Tel Aviv, Arab spectators – all as excited as we.

I gave these volunteers some advice which may not have been quite unnecessary.

"My friends, that you will be brave I know; but it is not the danger to life and limb which is the most difficult thing for a soldier to endure. Much more difficult are two other troubles of army life – monotony and rudeness. You see danger only once a month; but between attacks you must sit for weeks in the trenches, repeating again and again hateful, monotonous routine jobs, without any excitement, without any change – and then the sergeant, even your own sergeant, will add uncomplimentary appellations, like 'bloody fools' or its Hebrew equivalent. You must be able to stand this. Not the man who can shoot best is the best soldier. The best soldier is the man who can endure the most. And when the British N.C.O. swears, it does not mean that he is rude. The Englishman is our partner today, and to him, unlike us, life is a game. But perhaps his philosophy is also a useful one. For in sport the average man is more patient and more honest than in everyday life. A merchant may cheat his customer, but he will not cheat at cards. For at games, if not in life, everybody likes to be a gentleman. And you all remember how, as children, you used to play a game in which the loser had to get a fillip on the tip of his nose. Should anybody hit you on the tip of your nose in the street, you would hit back, but in play you swallow the blow and laugh. That is the Englishman's outlook. Everything is a game, especially war. The sergeant swears at you? It is only a playful fillip; don't be annoyed. You have to flounder in deep mud? Regard it as a bad card in a game; have patience. A bullet, a bomb? It is also a part of the game. I do not believe in their philosophy generally, but in war it is best – play the game like good players, and hold on...."

Before I left Tel Aviv I saw Weizmann. He was excited and somewhat dissatisfied.

"You have cleaned out the country," he said to James Rothschild. "Where are we to find workers and teachers and officials?"

But later, when the volunteers had to leave to do their military exercises, he attended a grand parade and, presenting them with a Jewish flag, made a moving speech; he thanked them in the name of the Jewish people for this colossal manifestation, which must help to strengthen the Jewish claim on Palestine, and wished them success and victory. But I neither saw nor heard this, and only read of it in a letter in the trenches.

A section of the volunteer movement was left out of the celebration – the girls. They had themselves not ventured seriously to hope that there would be a division of "Amazons," but they had earnestly expected that a "Red Magen David" detachment would be created.

This was formed only much later and on a small scale. A small number was accepted for hospital service – but only such as had already had some experience, for it was too late to train inexperienced nurses. This small group was officially recognized as the Jewish "Red Cross" and was attached to the Legion. Their official name and insignia were the Red Magen David. They all served together in the military hospital at Belah on the Egypt-Palestine border, near the big camp of Rafah where one of the three Jewish battalions was always stationed after the armistice.

They made admirable nurses, yet I do not mind boasting that they were "admired" also in the other sense. Partly at least, we Jews are still a people of the East, with some of its characteristics, and I fear that some of my readers will therefore consider the incident I am about to relate as unnecessary. But I do not believe in these characteristics. I believe that we are both the children and the active co-creators of European culture, one of whose virtues is its pride in the glory of womanly attractiveness. I remember that at the time of the first meetings of the League of Nations at Geneva, the whole of the World Press commented on a clever trick the British delegation played – bringing along only such typists as were outstandingly pretty. English womankind, on the whole, are hardly more beautiful than the average of other nations. But for Geneva a special selection was made. And rightly so. For this is also a part of national pride.

The incident occurred at the Rafah camp near Belah Hospital, where our Red Magen David group was serving. The Anzacs arranged a race meeting and invited our battalion. Colonel Patterson brought along two of the Jewish nurses. There were many other women present, English nurses with their matron, extremely striking in their uniforms, and many of them members of English society. In the interval, however, a group of men gathered around our nurses; the Anzac General Chaytor, his staff, his colonels and majors and lieutenants, about fifty in all, pushed us all aside, including myself (except Colonel Patterson who believes nobody may deprive an Irishman of his position near a young woman), and practically the whole half hour of the interval was spent in happy conversation, jokes and compliments.

For the Yishuv had both strong men and good-looking women. We may be proud of both.

The last months of the war were happy ones for the Palestine Yishuv. They had lived through terrible years. Of the estimated sixty thousand Jews in Jerusalem before the war there remained but twenty-three thousand. Only a small number had been able to emigrate; more than twenty-five thousand had died of starvation and disease. Even in March, 1918, four months after the capture of Jerusalem, poverty was visible in the Holy City. Children were begging for bread in the streets. "Don't give me money if you don't want to – buy me some bread," they would cry. Jewish children as beggars was something new for Jerusalem. Before the War one could find Jewish beggars only at the Wailing Wall. Even the *haluka* Jews never begged in the streets, keeping their sons from morning to night in *heder* and their daughters at home. But hunger makes great changes.

A tragedy more bitter than hunger played itself out in the final year of Turkish domination. They call it the *Rigul* (espionage). A strong, talented man, great in his virtues and great in his failings, built up, under the nose of Jemal Pasha and his Turkish and German staff officers a secret organization for supplying the British with information about the situation in the country and within the Turkish Army. He established contact between his headquarters in Palestine and the British H.Q. in Egypt; on several occasions British submarines brought his agents to Port Said and back. The British say that this organization assisted them materially in their victory; but the better part of the Yishuv for many years could not speak of it except with hatred and abhorrence. I cannot judge who are in the right. But I can say two things: among those who participated in the "espionage" were figures of epic determination, of romantic preparedness to hazard, ready, if necessary, to make the supreme sacrifice. I hope that the bard will yet arise to sing of those days, of those people, with their misdeeds and their noble heroism, with their irresponsibility and their undaunted bravery. Secondly, I know that the "espionage" activities brought much pain to the Yishuv. Sarah Aronson, whom the Turks tortured with medieval brutality for two whole days in Zikhron Yaakov, by beating her with bamboo sticks, by placing hot boiled eggs under her armpits, and by the devil knows what else, until she shot herself under their eyes without disclosing a word of information; and the two or three young men who were hanged in the marketplace of Damascus, were not the only sacrifices of the movement. Arrests and searches were the order of the day throughout the whole country, from Dan to Beersheba. There are numbers of people in Palestine today, completely innocent, who had their soles beaten for hours on end, or their hands twisted, or their fingers broken – for information. It was a period of terrible, inhuman terror.

Then, suddenly, on the second of November, 1917, there came the noise of the first cannon-shots of Allenby's attack on Gaza; in but a few weeks the South and the whole of Judea, from Jerusalem to Petah Tikva and Jaffa, were free. And the Yishuv learned that on that very second of November, the world had heard the thunder of another cannon, the Balfour Declaration, directed against the old fortress of Exile, and that the Jewish Army, about which they were hearing so many vague stories, was already coming to conquer Samaria, Galilee, Eastern Palestine...the sun of messianic redemption had risen!

You who live in gigantic cities will find it difficult to imagine what atmosphere was thus created in the Yishuv. They were altogether about fifty thousand souls. When a tremendous wave of spirited enthusiasm sweeps over a small community, one sees phenomena which are nothing short of wonderful. Perhaps this was one of the secrets of ancient Athens, in that remarkable century which saw Pericles, Socrates and Sophocles, when the freemen population of the city numbered no more than about thirty thousand. One cannot compare the Yishuv with Athens. But this may be said without hesitation. No city, not the largest in the world, possessed as large a number of idealists as the Yishuv in those days. They were a select number, not of the greatest but certainly of the most elevated spirits which Hibbat Zion and Herzl's Zionism gave to the Jewish people.

In nearly every cottage in Tel Aviv, in Zikhron Moshe of Jerusalem, in Rehovot, you could find men whose names had for twenty or thirty years been honorably bound up with the movement for Jewish liberation. They had suffered, at first enduring the jeers of skeptics, then material and spiritual poverty in a wild country, then the terrors of the war under Turkey. And they, just they, were privileged to see the first rays of light: before their eyes the last act of the Jewish tragedy was being enacted; it was in their houses that British generals were quartered, and it was their sons who were fighting on the Mountains of Ephraim and on the Jordan. Except perhaps for the days of Greece's struggle for independence a century ago, it is difficult to find an epoch of history in which there were intertwined to such a degree such traditions of antiquity, such memories of glory, such profundity of suffering and pain and such a blossoming of hope. A happy enthusiastic community awaited the coming of the British.

And yet it was a small Yishuv, where everybody knew everybody else and the smallest incidents were magnified a hundred-fold. The problem of arranging suitable accommodation for the ten members of the Zionist Commission occupied the attention of the whole "upper circle" of Jerusalem and Tel Aviv. People would come for miles to view the automobile of the Commission. Yigal, a young worker, broke through the Turkish lines, brought a message from Haifa and Galilee, told of excitement among the workers who had not volunteered for the Legion, excitement among the workers learning to shoot at Tel-el-Kebir in Egypt, excitement among the people of Jerusalem and Jaffa and in all the colonies. And then came the first Hadassah group from New York: Dr. Rubinow with thirty doctors and nurses, with packages of medicines, with a convoy from America, a joyful boon for those days and a promise of great deeds to be done, of millions and billions of dollars to come for the upbuilding of the Jewish state.

There was much exaggeration in that atmosphere: "dangers" would be seen in every shadow – and just where dangers did not lurk. Jewish girls were seen walking with Australian soldiers – *a danger for the morals!* Poor Jews opened up tea-rooms and sold cakes to Englishmen – *a danger that the Yishuv would become a community of hotel and restaurant servants for tourists. "We don't want to make another Switzerland!"* The "upper circle" hid its German and French books which remained from Turkish times, and learned to say "All right" and "How do you do?" – *English assimilation.* The atmosphere was slightly puritanical, but it did not matter. It did not materially disturb the spirit of jubilation.

I breathed this atmosphere only at intervals, in short, hurried journeys between Egypt and the battalion's headquarters. Yet I have never in my life breathed in an atmosphere of such pure, clean, child-like joy. All this was in spring.

In October, on our return from Transjordan, after the triumph of the Allies on all fronts, the atmosphere had changed completely.

Chapter XI

Our First Front

The actual military history of our battalion falls into three parts: the summer months at the front at Shechem, the great offensive in the Jordan Valley, and the Armistice.

The first of these periods was comparatively quiet. After the terrific tussle of the preceding winter, which had resulted in the liberation of Southern Palestine from Turkish domination, both sides decided to rest. The Turks in particular were not at all keen on taking the initiative, and the few small clashes that took place during those months were all local English attacks.

Many of my readers probably saw the war themselves from within, but perhaps they are not all acquainted with the methods of modern warfare in hill country. Our front was midway between Jerusalem and Shechem (Nablus). As you drive from Jerusalem to Shechem you come to a village, El Bira (the ancient Be'erot Binyamin mentioned in the Second Book of Samuel), and then to Ein Sinia (the ancient Yeshana). Immediately beyond, you turn left from the road to the narrow valley known to the Arabs as Wadi-Ed-Jib. Here between two deserted Arab villages, Abouein to the left and Jiljilia (one of the many places referred to as Gilgal in the Bible) to the right, was our first front.

Imagine a long chain of hills, about 2,500 feet high, running from west to east. North of the hills is a deep valley, and on the other side of this valley a second parallel chain of hills even higher than the first. We were encamped on the first and the Turks on the second. The distance between the summits of the hills was about two miles. We could not see the Turkish camp even with the aid of field-glasses, for they were encamped two hundred feet below the summit on the far side of their hill. During the day we were not permitted to move about on the top of the hill, and the guards were stationed at rocky observation posts. At night a strong guard was sent out to the other side of the hill, and they stationed themselves behind low stone fences called sangars; in addition, a patrol would descend nightly into the valley and stay there throughout the night, in order to warn us in case of attack.

It was a peaceful time, the right thing for introducing raw recruits to the atmosphere of war. Every morning the Turks would give us the pleasure of half an hour's bombardment, but they always displayed a marked predilection for a deserted hill far to our right and much higher up, and at least one-third of their shells did not even explode. They really fired at our position only three or four times, but they could not hit us. The hills there do not rise precipitously, but gradually, in terraces about as wide as East Broadway in New York. One day these terraces may be used for agricultural purposes. We used the highest of them for other purposes. Our tents were clustered together beneath the shelter of the summit. Our position was thus rendered inaccessible to the shells of the enemy. Probably ours were just as ineffective, but we did not waste so many.

The war we conducted is regarded as "small warfare." We knew nothing of the modern scientific horrors. It was seldom that we saw an airplane duel, in which both machines circled around one spot like the horses in a roundabout, firing at each other and bedecking the sky with small white cloudlets with all the soft beauty of sheep-wool.

We also knew nothing of gas. True, in mid-July, we suddenly had "gas exercises" introduced. We were compelled to adjust heavy anti-gas contrivances to our stomachs and to wear them all day, and every morning we rehearsed the adjustment of gas masks. We were told that this had to be done because of the receipt of information that the Turks had begun gas exercises. Later on, when we asked some of the captured Turkish officers what the reason was for their gas exercises, they told us, "We were told that the English had begun gas exercises."

The men had only two dangers to face during those months: night patrol duty and the seven days' watch at Abouein.

Eight to twelve men would go out on night patrol under a lieutenant. They would swathe their heavy military boots in thick rags, to lessen their noise; their knees were also covered with rags, for in the summer we wore shorts, and the hills were covered with a tremendous variety of prickly vegetation. Before the departure of the patrol the officer would receive a sealed envelope from the commander of the battalion, containing an exact description of the path to be taken by the patrol that night. Very often it was not just a stroll through the valley, but also a climb up to the enemy's hill – sometimes to within two hundred feet of his observation post. It was no light task. First there was the climb down our hill, over stones and through thorny grass, guns in hand – without noise. This took more than an hour. Then we had to creep about in the valley, one mile to the right and one mile to the left, among the bushes – hastily consulting the sergeant to decide whether some dark object we had seen was a Turk or just a cactus bush. Then came the most difficult part: the climb up the enemy's hill, finding our way with the aid of a compass and with the help of such directions as "left of a split fig tree," "ten paces to the right from a ditch," or, finally, "reaching a rock fifteen feet high, which, looked at from the north, has the appearance of the head of a hippopotamus"! Who of us had ever seen a hippopotamus, let alone at such close quarters as to be able to recognize its profile in the dark? Here we rested, and the men were given slabs of chocolate. And then, back again down the hill for a two hours' climb. You are tired and footsore, and close to the enemy, and every step forward releases a whole avalanche of stones. Suddenly you hear a shot from somewhere, close behind the last man in the file. You whisper fiercely, "Down!" The whole patrol goes down. And you see, a hundred yards away, a small point of fire leaping into the air; it resolves itself into a rocket which sheds a rosy light over a long stretch of bushes, dry river bed, and rocks and holes in the valley.

It would be a most beautiful sight – if you could set your mind on it. That was the Turkish patrol. Then your own battalion takes your part. From Abouein, from Jiljilia and from the sangars, there breaks out a wild concert of rifle fire; and a moment later, from somewhere in the distance, the English artillery joins the chorus. Like a railway train at night in the Swiss Alps, a fiery comet makes its majestic way over your head and with a thundering noise explodes on the enemy hill.

Then another. And all for your sake! You would feel really honored – if you could set your mind on it. The tumult lasts half an hour; then silence descends again, and we climb and creep and climb again until we reach camp – and a dixie of steaming hot tea, sweet and delicious.

The other danger spot was Abouein. Although it was really in No Man's Land, it had been included in our line. As you descend our hill on the side nearer the Turks, you encounter, three hundred feet down, a kind of outcrop of the hill, in the shape of a great terrace or "table." On this table the Arabs had built a village of about fifty houses. "Abouein" means "two fathers"; I cannot recall its being mentioned either in the Bible or in the Talmud. Yet it must have been far from poor, if one judges by the ruins that we found.

Each week a new platoon would be sent to Abouein, which it had to occupy for seven days. During the day, of course, nobody could go between the village and the camp, as the intervening ground was visible to the enemy. We therefore went at night. But between the observation post in Abouein and the Battalion headquarters we had a field telephone, through which we could sometimes hear one or two words of what was being said at the other end. Through this article of civilization we could "order" whatever we wanted from the Battalion – matches, tobacco, quinine, bandages, ammunition and letters – if there were any; and at night a small party of soldiers would bring six small mules laden with what was needed – or what they had understood was needed!

I have at home several letters which I wrote from Abouein. I shall translate a few extracts from them:

"Everybody has two childhood dreams: one is to be a king, or at least a governor, and the other is to see a Moslem harem from within. I have had both these dreams fulfilled. For seven days I am the governor of Abouein, can give whatever orders I like, can destroy the whole village if I so desire (and if I am prepared to face a court-martial on the eighth day); and I am living in a harem, with thick wooden bars in the windows. The pleasure is somewhat dampened by the fact that the ladies of the harem are elsewhere, and that the other residents are only members of my platoon; still, it's an interesting experience."

"... In truth we live here only at night. As soon as darkness falls, we place the watch at their different points overlooking the valley, and a quarter of an hour later fiery Corporal Salomon, head of Observation Post Number Two, must be told to find out whether he is shooting at the Turks or at the patrol coming from our camp. Then we begin our 'constructive' work. The colonel has given instructions to repair the barbed wire where Turkish bombs have torn it up and to add layers of bricks to the wall behind which we shelter when relieving the telephone operator at the observation-post: the wall is too low and the colonel is afraid that the far-sighted Turkish eye may distinguish a yellow helmet from yellow rocks at a distance of two miles. I therefore take those men who are not on guard – or who are not malaria-stricken – and together we fulfill the injunction of building up the country."

"... Hurrah! We have conquered the malaria. When I wrote you that my kingdom had no denizens, I was referring to humans. But there are other inhabitants who have remained in Abouein – in their millions! Never in my life did I dream that there were so many mosquitoes on this earth. Before sunset we cover our bare knees and rub a kind of oil into our hands, face and neck; but to the little beast this stuff has all the attraction of sweetmeats, and they bite with such elevated enthusiasm that one gets tired of scratching. The result: on the first morning two men went down with malaria. I held a council of war with Sergeant Fineman, who also lives in my harem, and we decided to drive out the winged inhabitants of the town in the wake of their human predecessors. I instructed the telephone operator to order two big barrels of paraffin, and Corporals Stukelin and Israel – the former is one of the best of the converts, and the latter is again with us after having spent two weeks in the cells for a brawl in the canteen – were instructed to crawl about all day, from house to house and from hole to hole, in order to find and register all damp spots likely to be the abodes of mosquitoes. With all my respect for our 'tailors,' of whom I am a great admirer, this was a task of outstanding importance which could be entrusted only to Zion Mule Corps boys. Late in the evening they returned from their expedition, dusty and dirty from head to foot with crawling about on the ground (for walking upright is forbidden); but they brought with them the addresses of three headquarters.

"Later that night the blessed Battalion mules brought the paraffin – by a heavenly miracle the telephone operator had been rightly understood at the Battalion end. With much ceremony we went off to make the enemy's position untenable. The mosquitoes made a monster counterattack – this was three days ago, and I am still bitten all over. But tonight there is no more than a meager platoon of lonely, gloomy mosquitoes, flying about silently, and lacking appetite not only for our blood but even for our ointment…."

"…Every day I grow to admire our 'tailors' more and more. Yesterday was a red-letter day. Rishon colonists sent us a gift, which required two mules to carry: grapes, figs, apple pie and date pudding. I have a suspicion that there was wine as well, but H.Q. must have decided that wine is unhealthy for men stationed in No Man's Land…. About midday, when the platoon had had a refreshing sleep after a hard night's work, the sergeant distributed the good things. We are all living in one house, the sergeant and I on the second floor and the men in three large rooms underneath. The Turks can see only our roof, so I allow the men to sit in the courtyard. Usually they play cards – I hope not for money, for this is against regulations. Today they were also sitting in shady corners of the yard, eating their grapes and playing some game or other – when suddenly the Turk opened a symphony of cannon music. Though he seldom shoots in the daytime, we are well acquainted with his firing: he always directs it at the lofty, totally deserted hill to our right. I immersed myself further in my book, and the boys in the yard went on with their game. But five minutes later the sergeant came in to me. 'I am afraid, sir,' he said, 'that they're trying to hit us. The sound is different from the usual. They're groping for Abouein.' And indeed the next shell exploded almost in the village. I put my head out through the window and shouted, 'Take cover!' They had heard what was happening themselves, but they did not relish the idea of interrupting their game to go into the gloomy Arab rooms. Slowly, reproachful at my repeating the order, they separated, carrying their cards and grapes and bits of apple tart in their hands. We waited. Every five minutes an explosion came, first to our right, then to our left, then right again.... 'Their shooting is pretty bad,' said the sergeant. He was standing by the window. Suddenly he smiled and beckoned to me. I walked over to him and looked out into the yard. Four of our boys were again sitting outside, absorbed in their cards and their date pudding, but they were in a corner which could be seen only with difficulty from the window. Suddenly one of them glanced around and quickly said in Yiddish, 'The officer's watching!' And just at that moment a shell burst right in Abouein, a hundred yards from us. I saw three of them raise their heads, but they did not budge; the fourth didn't even turn his head; he banged his card down on his opponent's – and replied with a note characteristic of deeply absorbed card players: "*Hob ich ihm in dr'erd.*" (I hope he meant the shell, not the officer.) I looked stern and made them take cover again; but inwardly I am proud of my 'tailors.'"

"... Is the Jew disciplined or not? A difficult question to answer.... Here you have an example. English and Australian soldiers destroyed so many trees (unfortunately from our Herzl Forest as well) that an order had to be sent out forbidding the cutting down of trees on penalty of a substantial fine. Here, around Abouein, are thick woods, and we need wood for cooking. But never will it occur to our men to touch a tree. They know well that I would not make inquiries as to the origin of their wood – for life in No Man's Land is hard enough in all conscience. But they are townsmen, brought up with the idea that a tree is communal property which dare not be hurt, just as one does not destroy a monument. Where do they find fuel? Doors, windows, or they break up the roof of a hut and take out the twigs and roots with which the *fellahin* make their roofs. But a tree? God forbid."

Chapter XII

Sodom and Gomorrah at Close Quarters

After a month on the Shechem front and two weeks' rest we were sent to the Jordan Valley.

It was the middle of August, 1918. We were there for five weeks – and then began the great offensive. Then a further two weeks' march, in the terrific heat of the hottest region created by God in the countries on the Mediterranean Sea.

The reader should understand that the Jordan Valley at Jericho and the Dead Sea is one of the deepest spots in the world, being 1,200 feet below sea level.

The climate of Palestine is generally regarded as subtropical, something like Florida or California; in the higher parts, especially in Jerusalem and Safed, the winter is often very cold – in 1920, Jerusalem lay for three days under snow. I do not remember a heavier fall than this even in St. Petersburg. But for the climate of the Jordan Valley even "tropical" would be too mild a description. The contrast is tremendous, unbelievable. While the snow was thick in Jerusalem, roses were blossoming in Jericho – and the distance between Jerusalem and Jericho can be covered in an hour and a quarter by motorcar.

In summer, it is a purgatory. In a town like Jericho, the heat may be endured, for you can shut yourself up in a windowless and almost doorless Arab house. But outside – Gehenna! Even the Bedouins usually absent themselves for two months between mid-July and September, just at the time that our men were stationed in the Mellaha, close to Jericho and the Dead Sea – not far, if you like, from Sodom and Gomorrah.

Patterson writes in his book that no other white battalions (except for cavalry) were ever made to remain there for more than a couple of weeks. I have heard the same. I do not reproach the General Staff for our having been kept there for almost two months, and I am certain that neither the Londoners nor our American men (for Colonel Margolin's two companies, composed mainly of Americans, were there) regret that they fought in the Jordan Valley. I have been told over and over again, by old experienced officers, absolute strangers, that those two months in the worst and deepest hole on the whole world front were in themselves a first-class military achievement, which can be compared to any of the famous fights of endurance in the history of all the armies in the war.

But even in the Jordan Valley there is no place so waste as the Mellaha. It is a narrow valley, running parallel with the Jordan and lacking even the slightest trace of vegetation. The earth is whitish-gray, salty and bitter to the tongue – perhaps a treasure house for the chemist of the future. Down the middle of the valley flows a narrow stream of salt water – one yard wide, but sufficient to poison the whole of the surrounding country with miasmas of malaria.

Those who have a palate for tragic beauty, for destruction and everlasting death, may here feast their eyes to satiety. The same white-gray hills on all sides – each looking like a heap of dirty salt, mixed with alkali and saltpeter, each reminding us of the fate of Sodom and Gomorrah. And if you venture to climb onto one of these hills you see about you something inexorably reminiscent of some ancient, early-biblical world catastrophe: unnaturally twisted, mutilated rocks (on one of which the Christians believe the Devil to have had his forty-day debate with the Nazarene) and a yellowish naked waste, eternally disturbed by dusty whirlwinds.

How goodly are thy tents O Jacob, thy dwellings O Israel! Here our tents were pitched. True, the American companies had a better camping spot – to the west of the Mellaha, in the valley of the Audja stream, whose water is sweet and whose banks were first of all lined with rocks to prevent the formation of swampy pools which might become the cradle of the malaria mosquitoes. But with us in the Mellaha, malaria reigned supreme. Every evening we used to watch a procession of camels, sometimes ten, sometimes fifteen or twenty, moving along the valley with their soft dignified tread, bearing a stretcher on each side, and in each stretcher one of our stricken comrades. Our battalion consisted of 800 men when it arrived in the Jordan Valley; when the offensive was launched there remained but 550; when we returned victorious to Lod there were some 150 and of our thirty officers there were only about fifteen left. More than twenty men were killed, wounded or captured. The rest were down with malaria. Later, thank God, most of them came out of hospital, thin and pale, but well; more than thirty lie buried on the Mount of Olives.

We were not troubled by Turkish bombardment, though Margolin's companies farther south suffered much from a big Turkish cannon which the men called "Jericho Jane." But patrol service became a dangerous joke. The southern part of the Jordan Valley, where we were, is a broad and deep canyon, but through its middle runs a narrow stream near which the Jordan flows. The Turks still held both banks of the Jordan.

The work of our patrols was not only to watch for an attack, but to find the best path to the stream. This entailed traversing long distances every night, and it was a most difficult task, for it meant evading both the Turkish patrols and their observation posts – stealing between two Turkish forts on both journeys. Almost every night we would hear a volley of shots from somewhere along the line. On the third night we lost our Sergeant Levy, an English Jew, whom I had known when we were both privates in the Twentieth London Regiment, and who had asked to be transferred to the Legion. His comrades were unable even to find his body in the darkness, and returned to our lines bearing two other wounded men. The colonel immediately called for volunteers to search for the sergeant. Sepiashvili, one of the Georgian Jews to whom I have often referred, went out with three others. They must have been seen by the enemy, for shortly after their departure the concert of rifle-music was resumed. But three hours later Sepiashvili brought back the dead body of the sergeant. Thus did the young son of a small Caucasian Jewish family win the first decoration for our regiment. Sergeant Levy was not the only one who died on patrol service in the Jordan Valley – but when the time for the offensive came, many of our lieutenants and sergeants had a thorough knowledge of the paths leading from the Mellaha to the Jordan.

The peculiarity of our position in the Jordan Valley was that we were situated just at the cornerstone of the whole British line – the pivotal position. If you look at the map you can imagine the British front as a horizontal line starting from the sea just north of Petah Tikva, running over Abouein and Jiljilia to the Dead Sea. This sector, where the horizontal line suddenly turns down vertically, was occupied solely by us. In war such a "cornerstone" is just as important as in a building. It is the most favored point of attack, for two easily comprehensible reasons. When attacking one must be particularly careful of that kind of counter-attack known as "enfilade," that is, being attacked from the left or right flank. But this happens only when you have broken into a straight enemy line – then you have the enemy on both flanks and you can be enfiladed from both sides. But if you break through the enemy line at a corner you have the enemy only on one flank. It is incomparably easier and it is incomparably more worthwhile, for if you have broken through the corner your position is not only behind one but behind two of the enemy lines and you are able to attack them both from the rear. That is why it is said that a cornerstone position attracts the enemy as a tree attracts lightning.

Our position was made even more dangerous by the fact that we were left almost entirely without artillery support. As part of a secret plan, Allenby concentrated all his cannon in the Jaffa district, in order to direct the decisive blow. The results demonstrated the excellence of the plan, but in the meantime, both we and the Anzac cavalry divisions, which were stationed just behind us in the valley, were left without cannon cover. At the same time, our Intelligence Service conveyed the information that the Turks had seventy cannon in Transjordan. What all this meant was clear. We held both the weakest and the most dangerous position in the British line, at the most trying period of summer heat, and on top of it all, at the decisive moment of the campaign. Again: I have no reproaches. Commandant Levi-Bianchini, an officer of great experience, whom the Italian Government sent as its representative on the Zionist Commission, said afterward, "With all my respect both to the Jewish battalion and to Allenby, I should not have sent men with only three months' service to such a point; he probably had a high opinion of your boys."

I am inclined to believe that at that time Allenby's opinion of our record was a first-class one. Our patrols often used to steal up to the observation posts of the enemy, and they gleaned much useful information regarding the composition of the Turkish front, for which Allenby's Headquarters once sent a special letter of thanks to one of our officers, Lieutenant Abrahams. Then, the percentage of malaria defections among us (before we entered the Jordan Valley), was the lowest of all the regiments – another confirmation of an oft-asserted truth, that the Jew, despite the fact that his muscles and chest are less developed, has yet a more healthy constitution than the average Gentile. There was a further fact which probably played its part: we were the one white battalion which had no drunkards in its ranks! In Portsmouth our canteen had had to be closed down for lack of patronage. The army and the world in general usually laugh at the man who refuses to "have another." But in a moment of crisis one is forced to reckon with the fact that here was a peculiar battalion whose whole manpower could be relied on, even on a holiday.

And there was another reason: no other battalion caught as many Turkish prisoners as ours. I admit that this was due to something other than superior heroism: again the Zion Mule Corps boys. Nearly all of them knew Arabic and several knew Turkish. At every clash with the Turkish patrols, they would call out to the Turkish soldiers, "Come to us – we'll give you food!" This was an important matter for the Turks. Both their army and their country were highly disorganized. The men had to live for long periods on dry bread and on God's fresh air.

Within a week the rumor spread in the Turkish ranks that there were friends among the Jews who spoke Turkish and who promised good things.... There were days when our patrol would bring back six or more prisoners.

Yes, in those days General Allenby seemed to have a good opinion of Jewish soldiers. He wrote a letter to the colonel promising the formation of a Jewish Brigade with Patterson as general.

When one must, one forgets personal prejudices and one does not even heed bad advice. Then one reckons purely with the objective worth of men as men. But once that moment passes, everything is changed.

Chapter XIII

Beyond the Jordan

On the nineteenth of September, General Chaytor, commander of the Australian and New Zealand cavalry forces and of all the forces in Transjordan, summoned Colonel Patterson and gave him his instructions for the offensive. Our battalion, together with Margolin's two companies, was to form what would be known as "Patterson's Column." Its first task would be to capture both sides of the ford across the Jordan known to the Arabs as Umm Esh Shert, and thereafter to advance on the town of Es Salt in the Hills of Moab, far beyond the Jordan.

Collecting the various units of the battalion occupied an entire night. Our line stretched for a distance of nine or ten miles, concentrated on seven small mountain forts which formed a chain from north to south.

That same night we sent out reinforced patrols to No Man's Land, to find out whether the Turks were still in their forts, for after the blow they had suffered several days earlier at Jaffa, they had begun to retreat from the Jordan as well.

The patrols found only two forts occupied. As we had no artillery, we opened up machine-gun fire on them. They replied. At three o'clock in the morning they again became silent. But the patrols brought back the information that the "ditch" – the deepest part of the valley, where the Jordan flows – was occupied by heavy troops on both sides of the river.

Two days later we were already stationed in a long line at the edge of the ditch, and we could look out carefully, over the ridge of improvised trenches, at the Jordan itself. The ditch in that part, if I remember rightly, is about a mile wide, thickly covered with woods and bush on both sides, and its depth is about two hundred feet.

The rocks prevented our seeing whether the woods were occupied, but at night our patrols informed us that movements could still be heard in the thick growth.

On the morning of the twenty-second of September, one of our companies whose position was at the north end of our line sent out a small party of men to drive away the enemy from the portion of the wood lying directly under their sector of the ridge. They were led by Lieutenant Cross, a Jew, and he had with him our transport officer, the Irish Captain Julian, who wished to see the ground over which he would soon have to bring his camels and mules.

At about two o'clock, Colonel Patterson was informed that the party had been ambushed by Turks armed with machine guns, and that Lieutenant Cross had been wounded and taken prisoner, and Captain Julian wounded. He would have remained lying where he fell had not one of the men dragged him away in the midst of a hail of bullets. I do not remember the name of the gallant man, but he received a decoration.

Incidentally, there is a well-known Jewish anecdote about a soldier who was continually dragging away wounded officers under fire and who explained himself thus, "If they shoot, they'll hit him and not me." On the foundation provided by this story, which is widely spread among Jewish gossips, many believe (I have heard it from their own lips) that rescuing wounded men is the best method of defense under fire. Jews are usually inclined to formulate their opinions on the basis of some humorous anecdote. The only method of defense under fire is to hide behind a tree, a rock, a mound, or if there is no cover at all, simply to throw oneself flat on the ground and remain perfectly still. To go dragging others about means simply to forego this protection; anybody daring to do so must have courage and strong nerves – and that man honestly won his medal.

But our attempt at taking the "ditch" failed.

On the twenty-third my company was ordered to make the second attempt to gain the ford at Umm Esh Shert and to drive away the last Turks from the right bank of the river for a distance of about a mile. We were to do so that night and achieve our purpose at all costs.

The Jordan, in its southern part, is very deep and flows with that extraordinary swiftness which makes it beloved of hydroelectric engineers. Even cavalry can cross it only at the Umm Esh Shert ford. For anybody on foot even the ford was impossible, it being too deep and the river flowing too fast. But General Chaytor's dragoons were awaiting the capture of Umm Esh Shert in order to be able to enter Transjordan, and we were ordered to effect the capture.

Malaria had robbed my company of all but three officers and less than a hundred men. Lieutenant Barnes was in charge and I was temporarily second-in-command. Abrahams had to take over the work of the other three platoon commanders. Barnes and Abrahams occupied the rocks with seven of our eight Lewis guns. I was given the remaining Lewis gun and was ordered to conduct the main operation. There was nothing praiseworthy about our work: the plan had been carefully worked out by the colonel and we just had to carry it out. I describe the operation here only because it was mentioned in Allenby's dispatches, and also because it was my last real military experience: though I must admit that in comparison with the patrol service which had preceded it, it was child's play.

At midnight we left the ridge and proceeded in marching order directly to Umm Esh Shert. We did not creep but marched upright along the wide Turkish road, for we had seen during the day that the ford, at any rate on our side of the river, was unoccupied. A hundred paces from the hills we halted and sent out scouts to reconnoiter. They returned with the news that the road was clear. We brought down our Lewis gun to the bank and took up our position on an elevated piece of ground opposite the ford. The gun was placed in a position covering both banks of the river. But the ford was clear on the other side as well. The Jordan at this point is about as broad as Park Avenue in New York; both approaches to the ford were clear of all vegetation. The night was not very dark and it was possible to see with our field-glasses that there was nobody at the stream. I left Sergeant Moskow with twenty men, and with the rest we went to comb the woods near our bank of the stream.

This was more difficult. The trees are not tall, but they are close up to one another, and the ground is covered with all manner of thorns and similar vegetation. Two men, one from the Zion Mule Corps, the other a Londoner, marched ahead; twenty paces behind them the party followed in a long, widely-spread line, reaching from the banks to the rocks which are the boundary of the Jordan "ditch" on the west. The company was thus enabled to make a thorough search in the woods.

Only once did we hear shots, but they came from the other side of the river. We did not reply. I signaled to Barnes, however, indicating the spot where the shots came from, and he opened fire with his Lewis guns. For five minutes the enemy replied; then there was silence. It was probably the rear-guard of the retreating Turks.

Shortly before sunset my scouts encountered the scouts of another of our companies, which had reconnoitered the upper portion of the "ditch," going in the opposite direction, southward. I signaled that the ford was free; the colonel telephoned to General Chaytor's staff, and an hour later the first dragoons could peacefully cross the Jordan and start pushing the retreating Turks away from the Land of Gilead. Allenby's report says, "On the night of 23rd September the Jewish battalions captured the Jordan ford at Umm Esh Shert." The ford, the key to Transjordan, was given them by us – a curious commentary on the fact that today Transjordan is excluded from the Jewish National Home.

Among the first infantry troops that entered Transjordan on the heels of the Australian cavalry were Colonel Margolin's Americans. They crossed the Jordan at the bridge Gorania, several miles south of Umm Esh Shert, and marched to Es Salt (believed to be the ancient Ramat Gilead), where Colonel Margolin settled down as commander of the town and its neighborhood. Our battalion followed Margolin's two companies.

This march in Transjordan was the most difficult I have ever experienced; and not I alone. Patterson, who still remembered the Boer War in the hot African sun, at a time when war did not consist as today of months of waiting in trenches, but wholly of maneuvers and marches, himself said that he had never endured more painful progress.

The march from the river to the foot of the Hills of Moab was difficult enough, through a roadless desert where the Turks had burned the dry grass in their retreat, and the heavy black smoke in the windless heat lay so thick on the ground that our companies often lost sight of each other. But many times worse was the climb up the hills. It was about midday. The gradient of the hill was one in about twenty; what this means can be appreciated if one realizes that the maximum gradient on which motor traffic is permitted to travel in Europe is one in from ten to twelve. And the men and N.C.O.s had to carry, in addition to their rifles and ammunition, bulky kit-bags as large as a four-year-old child, packed chockful with shirts, socks, shoes and everything else kindly provided by His Majesty, including razors and tins of polish for polishing buttons. And, of course, water bottles, from which the water had long evaporated.

The officers, who had only kit-bags to carry, helped as much as they could. Each of us carried a rifle on each shoulder; but it was of little avail.

The dust on the hills was worse than the smoke in the valley had been. It hung over the ground without a breath of wind to disturb it, and instead of air we breathed and swallowed dust.

Man after man would fall out and throw himself down near a rock, with mouth wide open, unable to carry himself farther. "Now they'll laugh at us – Jewish heroes!" I thought to myself, almost ashamed – until I saw two English sergeants, tall, slim, athletic men, who had been sent to us a short time before to replace two of our malaria-stricken sergeants, sitting against a rock with their eyes closed, gasping like fish on dry land.

We were marching through beautiful grounds now. Upon those hills once roamed with her companions the daughter of Yiftah the Gileadite and bewailed her virginity. Below, under the meandering road, ran a sonorous brook called Wadi Nimrin in Arabic, Mei Nemerim (Tiger stream) in the Bible. But instead of tigers its banks were strewn with dead horses. To this day I do not know why the Turks killed so many horses in their hasty retreat.

The corpses were not the only things the Turks had left behind. Far below our path we saw the famous "Jericho Jane": the mighty cannon lay athwart across the stream; the waves splashed into her muzzle, and she merrily spat them out. We found whole untouched packages of ammunition of all kinds strewn over the hills. And this was nothing to all that the Turks had cast away. A party of dragoons whom we met told us that they had seen numbers of rifles and even revolvers lying on the very path we were traversing. But now they had disappeared. What had happened to them? Whither had they gone.

This "whither" is one of the greatest threats to our future in Palestine, and it is a threat about which no doubts can exist. Even we, who came forty-eight hours after the dragoons, saw high up in the hills, hundreds of Bedouin with heavily-loaded asses.... Transjordan is well provided with the most modern arms!

I caught one of the Bedouin in the act of collecting ammunition. I should have had him taken and sent to Jericho, but I was too much struck by the humor of the situation. It is not much use beating a cat which is finishing the last drops of milk after the other cats have drunk their fill and departed in peace. I took his ass and loaded it with the packs of some of the weaker men.

Incidentally, this ass was not only our single gain on that march but was also destined to provide us with much amusement.

First, the men, though dead tired, decided to give it a name. For that name I ask pardon of all the Cohens of our people. There were more than fifty men named Cohen in our battalion, and the officers asserted that their initials exhausted all the letters of the alphabet except X. The men decided, therefore, that the name of the ass should be "Cohen, X."

Second, the Bedouin was both educated and impudent: he demanded a receipt for the confiscated animal. My sergeant suggested that I should give him "one on the jaw." But at one stage in my life I studied law at a university, and that is enough to disturb any man's balance for the rest of his days: I gave him a receipt. He put it away carefully and took it along to the depot at Jericho, and for weeks afterward letters went back and forth between the General Staff Headquarters and our battalion relating to "Cohen, X."

Halfway to Es Salt we were ordered back, down into the valley. This happens often with the English: first climb up, then down, with no reason for either. In such cases they usually quote Tennyson's famous line, "Someone has blundered," causing six hundred of a crack Guards Regiment to die in the battle of Sevastopol. "It is the most typically English line in our whole poetry," says Patterson (who is Irish).

An end comes to everything. By about five o'clock the heat had subsided and when, half an hour later, it had been replaced by a refreshing coolness, the order was given to halt for the night. The men rushed down the rocks into the valley to bathe in the stream and to drink their fill of the fresh, cold water from the Mei Nemerim: a beautiful stream with green banks, typical of that part of the country, well-watered in comparison not only with the wilderness on the opposite side of the river but even with the whole of Western Palestine... but it is excluded from the Jewish National Home.

Half a day's march from Es Salt we were ordered back to the Jordan Valley to take charge of Turkish prisoners. I remember them well: a terribly emaciated, half-dead mob they were, tattered, muddy and weary – nine hundred Turks and two hundred Germans and Austrians.

Among the latter there were still traces of discipline. We provided them with a large tin of water, and they lined up and drank quietly, one after another. But we could not even give water to the Turks: nobody would wait his turn, each one pushed and fought with the rest – each one, and they were nine hundred! The two sergeants and twelve men whom the colonel had sent to supervise the drinking simply did not know what to do. In about a quarter of an hour hardly twenty had managed to have a few sips each – and more than a bucketful had been spilled in the tussle.

The colonel rode up to find out what all the noise was about.

"There's only one thing to be done," he said. "Make them go down to the stream, like Gideon's heroes, *lehavdil!*" (*Lehavdil* was one of his Hebrew gems.)

A distance of at least a mile separated our camp from the stream. But the colonel was right – it was the only thing to be done with men in that state. To the stream they had to go.

I walked over to the Germans, found two hundred ready-made Republicans.

"Is Germany still fighting?"

"Yes," I said.

"Then Kaiser Wilhelm is mad," said one.

"He was that from the beginning," came another growl.

"At any rate we're finished with the War."

"With the Kaiser too!"

"And with Franz!"

I did not reply; it was hardly my affair, I have little love for people who change their colors because of reverses.

What they told me about themselves, however, was interesting.

Three days in the wilderness without water; Bedouin who would come and steal your watch, your ring, sometimes even the shoes from your feet; malaria, and comrades who fell by the way gasping, "Leave me, let me die in peace."

"Barnes," said the colonel, how many men have you left in your company?"

"Eighteen fit, sir," said the company commander.

"Tonight you will take the prisoners back to Jericho."

And we escorted them over a distance of twelve miles, eighteen Jews with three officers as guard over nine hundred Turks and two hundred Germans who, unarmed as they were, could have exterminated us in five minutes. The prisoners straggled along in fours; our men were distributed on either side of them – in a line in which we were not only out of sight but even out of hearing of each other.

Our padre accompanied us – to see that we should treat the enemy humanely in his misfortune.

We dragged on endlessly, at the pace of old women, through the Jordan Valley – silent, except for the groans of those suffering from malaria headache, but there were many such. The Germans groaned, but the Turks wept like little children, or like the jackals which kept at our heels in the darkness.

The padre and I brought up the rear. Suddenly we heard, far away, a scream, a shout, a shot. We ran forward. A small group was standing by the roadside; a Turk was on the ground and over him stood one of our men, a Georgian "*shvili*," yelling at him in Turkish.

"Who shot?"

The "*shvili*" explained. The Turk did not want to go farther, wanted to die on the road. He had tried to frighten him by talking of Bedouin and jackals, but to no avail; so he shot into the air and said, "That's how I'll shoot you if you don't move." But even this was useless. "Take two other Turks and tell them to carry him," said my companion.

The "*shvili*'s" reply was curt: "They'll throw him away in the darkness."

The next column marching past was composed of Germans. We chose four of them who seemed to be stronger than the rest, the padre took their names and they had to carry the Turk to Jericho.

I went back, and again we straggled forward in silence. About a mile, then another shot, this time much farther in front. I shrugged my shoulders. The padre raised his foot to mount his donkey; I tugged him unceremoniously by the leg and told him: "Don't meddle. It is in front. Barnes is there, let him manage."

The padre whispered, and his voice shook: "What if…if they shoot him?"

The German who walked in front of us apparently understood English: he said loudly to his neighbor, "The only thing to do is shoot the stragglers. One cannot leave them here to starve to death and let the jackals gnaw off their ears."

The padre became quiet and looked intently to right and left. It was pitch dark, impossible to tell a stone from a bush.

On and on we dragged ourselves, all of us engrossed in one thought. Only a week ago all these men here were the awe and glory of the earth. And it is but a mere accident that it is we who lead them, and not the opposite. Many were the thoughts I had that night. I had seen the cathedral of Rheims under gunfire, a dogfight between airplanes in the sky, the *gueules cassées* and the German bombers over London, which soldiers from the front swore was worse than Ypres, for in Ypres at least there was no women's and children's sobbing amid the thunder of bursting bombs. All this was terrible, but nature also knows how to mutilate people and destroy cities. One thing nature cannot do: humiliate, defile an entire nation. This is the bitterest of all, and it is man's monopoly. I had lived in Berlin and Vienna and Constantinople, seen these same fragments of God's image and likeness, working and laughing, strolling with their girlfriends along the Prater and smoking narghiles in the bylanes of Galata. Often when someone publicly calls me a militarist, I remember that night and the road, and the Jordan Valley, in the shadow of that same Mount Nebo where Moses died with God's kiss on his lips; I remember and do not answer. There is nothing to answer.

Awesome is the life of a nation; hard the march through the desert. You can't stand it? Then lie down and die. Mankind is a regiment, too, only without a kind padre, and no one will carry you until Jericho. Go on and drag yourself as far as you can, hard toward yourself and your neighbor; or lie down and go down with your hope unfulfilled.

Chapter XIV

Why There Was Quiet in Palestine

The third period of our service – the Armistice period – I consider the most important. More: the main purpose of the creation of the Legion was not so much its participation in the war – though we naturally desired this – as its remaining as the garrison of Palestine after the war.

These dreamers, who were the fathers and rearers of the Legion idea, were far from being romanticists. All of us were realists. Has Rutenberg not shown this by the electrification of Palestine? Have not Meir Grossman and Jacob Landau shown this by the fact that any Jew in the remotest corner of the world knows every morning what is happening to his fellow Jews everywhere else? And Trumpeldor?... We undoubtedly attached great value to the Jews themselves playing a part in the conquest of their homeland. I shall go further and say that we all hoped that this part would be a much greater one than it came to be. Not of one and a half battalions did we dream when we started our work; and not of battalions which would appear on the front so late, when half the country had already been liberated. True, our Legion also played an important and useful part at the decisive moment in both the Palestine campaign and the World War, but we had dreamed of something more. We had dreamed of an army which would go through the whole of the desert campaign, in the footsteps of Moses.

But, realistically, we felt in our dreaming that even thirty thousand men would constitute at most one-fifth of the army necessary to conquer Palestine.

We knew from the very beginning that, given even a maximum of success, the Jewish Legion could be only a part of the Army of Conquest. But quite another matter was the question of the Army of Occupation. In this we saw the main purpose of the Jewish Legion. If there was to be no possibility of its being sufficiently large to win Palestine itself, it should be sufficiently strong – and this was our fundamental aim – to form the major portion of the garrison which would remain in Palestine after the conquest. A garrison need not be so large as a conquering army. For a small country like Palestine, not thirty, but twenty, or even fifteen thousand men would be sufficient to play the leading part in maintaining law and order. And it was important that it should play this part at the time when the various Powers were discussing the future of the occupied territories.

And I must again admit that in this too we succeeded to a far more modest degree than we had hoped. With the exception of one occasion – and indeed a most important and critical occasion, to which I shall refer – the Jewish Legion was never the major part of the Army of Occupation which remained in Palestine after the Armistice.

I am therefore far from overestimating. Nor, however, need we underestimate. In 1919 our Legion constituted a far larger proportion of the British Army in Palestine than in 1918. In the first place the Legion increased threefold during that time. Only one and a half battalions, with a nominal numerical strength of 1,500, actually took part in the campaign. The rest were still in training in Egypt. But by the beginning of 1919 we had more than 5,000 men in our three battalions. In the second place, the British Army was substantially decreased after the victory.

A large portion was sent to Syria and Southern Anatolia, while another was sent to Egypt. Then demobilization began – among the British first. I do not remember the exact figures, but I believe that the average number of soldiers in British uniform, including colored (mainly Indian) regiments, stationed in Palestine during 1919, was 30,000. Of this number we were one-sixth; of the most important division of the army, the infantry regiments, we constituted one-quarter; and of the white infantry regiments almost one-half. I mention this not in order to seek solace either for myself or for the reader, but because objectively this analysis is important in all military calculations. The English lay great stress on the difference between white and colored soldiers. They have faith in the Indian troops, but only to a degree. This degree can best be illustrated by the fact that all the *actual* officers, down to the second lieutenants, are exclusively white. The Hindus are given special rankings, like "Jemadar" and "Soubadar," but they are not given officer's rank. I have heard that this has now been altered. But it was so in 1919 and 1920. Only white troops were regarded as absolutely reliable. As in war, so in the occupation of territory, the infantry is the bulwark of the army. And in the white infantry, Jews were then – if I remember correctly – not far short of one-half.

There came a moment when the proportion was even greater. It was, as I have mentioned, a critical moment for Britain's position in the Near East. In the spring of 1919, unrest spread throughout the whole of Egypt. Nearly all the white troops, both infantry and cavalry, were transported to Egypt. Apart from the Indians and one British battalion in Jerusalem, only five thousand Jewish soldiers remained in the country.

The troubles in Egypt lasted two months. During those two months the Arabs of Palestine went through a period of incessant incitement. Every day they would hear the most fantastic rumors of alleged British defeats. They were told that Allenby had been killed, that the nationalists had captured Cairo, that Arabi Pasha (an Egyptian hero of the battle of Tel el Kebir of 1882) had risen from the grave, and so on, in an endless series. Every day there would steal into Palestine – by train or on horseback or on foot – various agitators, sent and paid by God knows whom, who would distribute themselves throughout the towns and villages, and deliver speeches in the cafés, or sometimes in the marketplaces, inciting the Arabs against the English and the Jews.

It was undeniably a dangerous period. The English governors themselves shook their troubled heads, bemoaning to us (I was then on the Zionist Commission) the inadequacy of the garrison which had been left in Palestine, moreover a garrison composed largely of Indian troops, themselves mainly Moslems and themselves concerned over the fate of Constantinople and the precarious position of the Caliphate.

Then it was that headquarters again remembered the Jewish Legion. At such a time what is most important is the defense of the nervous system of a country – the railway lines; and the railway lines were placed under the watch of Jews – from Romani in the Sinai Desert to Rafah on the Egyptian border, from Rafah through Gaza to Lod and Jaffa, from Lod to Haifa, from Haifa to the Sea of Galilee. At Jaffa and Haifa too, Jewish garrisons were stationed – at Jaffa the Americans, at Haifa the Palestinians. Only to Jerusalem was the Legion stubbornly denied access. An English battalion guarded Jerusalem, but the whole of the rest of the country was surrounded by a chain of Jewish soldiers.

And the result – two months of complete order and absolute peace.

When all is quiet, the chronicler suffers: there is nothing to write about. As long as the Legion was a visible force in Palestine there occurred not a single clash, despite what was happening in Egypt. Only when there remained of our Legion of five thousand only four hundred – only then were Trumpeldor and his comrades killed at Tel Hai, only then did the pogrom break out in Jerusalem. But these tragedies are not part of my story. I tell of the Legion, and just so long as the Legion existed all was quiet and peaceful – and the military chronicler had nothing to write about.

This I consider to have been the chief purpose of the Jewish Legion in Palestine. And it will be the chief purpose of that new Legion, for which one of the Zionist parties is today striving and will strive until it again succeeds: we must have a Legion, just in order that the military chronicler of the future shall have nothing to write about. The chronicler of the work of reconstruction – yes; the chronicler of cultural upbuilding – yes; but the chronicler of unrest and clashes – nothing, just as in 1919.

Here I must for a moment touch upon that question which is so prominent in Zionist discussions – is it true that a Jewish Legion would incite and provoke the Arabs? It is essential that a question of this nature should be treated honestly. When there is a community which refuses to hear of a Jewish "National Home," it is natural that every manifestation of Jewish activity and of Jewish presence irritates it. It is irritated more particularly by the immigration of Jews, by the growth of Jewish land possessions and by every phenomenon which indicates Jewish progress toward playing a leading role in the country – as, for example, a Jewish High Commissioner, or the ceremonious opening of a Hebrew University.

To this category also belongs a Jewish Legion. Nobody denies that our opponents were most dissatisfied at the presence of Jewish battalions in Palestine; and if tomorrow new battalions are formed they will again be dissatisfied. But it is not fair to say that because of this spirit of dissatisfaction we should wash our hands of the object which caused it. For should this spirit be sufficient ground for washing our hands of anything, we must forego Zionism itself.

To put the question honestly means to weigh both sides of it, the disadvantages as well as advantages. Every project presents a dark side, every important remedy contains within itself an element which, under other circumstances, would be poisonous. I believe emphatically that life is logical. Only Jews – at any rate the Jews of yesterday's generation, who still control our affairs – have a hatred of logic and despise theories. They will concern themselves only with facts. Very well, here are the facts. The Legion in 1919, five thousand Jewish soldiers in view everywhere – and there is peace in the land. Then in 1920, the Legion almost entirely disbanded – and we have the dark days of Tel Hai and a second Kishinev in Jerusalem.

One further comment – not on the attitude of the non-Jewish inhabitants to our legionaries, but, on the contrary – on the attitude of the latter to the non-Jewish inhabitants.

A garrison battalion placed in the position of our Legion in Palestine requires two qualities – strength and tact. Its duty is not a purely military one; it is diplomatic as well. And the most difficult aspect is this: when there is need of strength – when such an unfortunate contingency arises – this strength will be manifested by the men collectively, under the command of experienced and tried officers. But diplomacy and tact must be possessed by every man individually – in his conduct toward individuals in the street, in the café, in the marketplace, when he is buying oranges from a fruit vendor. And this can be attained only with three types of people: those who have been blessed with inherent tact, those whose whole principle of relationship with their fellow men is that of "holding aloof," or those who have gained particular experience in the tactful handling of natives – as, for instance, the British soldiers in India, who are given special training in this important sphere of "handling."

From this introduction it should be easy to understand that not all our men were able to stand the test brilliantly. The vast majority did maintain an absolutely correct attitude. That this contention is justified, the following incident abundantly illustrates. In 1919 the Arab Executive issued an order that a flood of complaints should be poured into Military Headquarters against the conduct of the Jewish soldiers; it began to "pour." Our three colonels instantly demanded that every single complaint should be thoroughly investigated, not only by the battalion but by the military police. It was soon made manifest that 99 per cent of the complaints were unjustified; within a month the complaint epidemic was over.

But there were exceptions – though, let me hasten to add, not very important ones. I remember not a single case of an Arab being killed or injured by a Jewish soldier, though this did happen, and not so seldom, with other regiments. The Australians razed to the ground an entire village, Sarafend – near Lod, and a stone's throw from Allenby's headquarters – and killed a number of Arabs (having previously, with due chivalry, sent the women and children away) in retaliation for the shooting of a comrade.

Not only did nothing of this kind happen with our men, but there were never even any serious clashes. There were cases of rudeness, of unnecessary arguments, of drunken brawling and other similar trifles – trifles, however, that should have been avoided.

Though I intend to speak frankly, I desire to attack none of my Legion comrades. But my observation led me to certain general conclusions, which may be of some value when the time comes for us to decide on our general policy of tact and tactics in Palestine.

Not a word of reproach can be addressed to two categories of our men: the intellectuals among the Palestine Volunteers, and the English boys – without exception.

The former, previously college students, members of labor parties, teachers, officials and colonists, maintained an attitude, just as today, of cordiality and friendliness without intimacy, an admirable attitude in every respect.

Of the English boys – they who were called, at first mockingly, later proudly, "the tailors," I shall write later when I discuss the various elements in the Legion; here I need only mention that they belonged to the "holding aloof" category. Punctiliously and properly they did their work and wrote home to their wives; not Palestine, nor Zionism, nor the Arabs interested them to the slightest degree. If a drunken Arab cursed them in the street, they would not even turn their heads.

The Americans – here was another story. That they should have any trouble with Arabs was an infrequent occurrence, but it did happen. And I was consistently given the impression (for I was often taken along to arbitrate, or to defend our men on these occasions) that it happened because of the strong Zionist feeling prevailing among the Americans. As opposed to the English boys, the Americans brought with them a strong, often feverish, interest in Palestine and in everything Palestinian. They were affected by everything, troubled by every trifle.

They regarded the non-Jewish inhabitants partly with contempt, partly with sympathy, but they did regard them, while the English simply ignored them. Because of this they often magnified the foolish vulgarism of a hooligan to the size of a blow to Jewish national honor, or a shot in an Arab village, which hurt nobody, to a danger to the whole Jewish people. It is obviously not difficult to be tactful when one is indifferent; far more difficult is it to maintain discretion when one deeply loves something. That is why my remarks are not a reproach; but facts are facts.

The real potential source of trouble, however, was the other section of the Palestine Volunteers, those who had themselves grown up in an Oriental environment. They did not dislike the Arab; on the contrary, they knew him, were friendly with him, and spoke his language as well as he did. And it was just this that brought about the majority and the most unpleasant of the clashes. Here is a typical picture of such a clash. One of these men, home on leave, meets an Arab acquaintance; they greet one another and kiss in true Oriental fashion; they go into a café, have drinks together and sit down to a game of cards; they twit each other, as friends will; they become sarcastically witty – and the result is an exchange of blows. Or, more often, something I have already mentioned: a drunken Arab drops a curse in the street. The fiery American may not always understand him, for he knows no Arabic. But this Jew understands Arabic, and can, moreover, reply in the same tongue. He stops in his stride and launches his reply. The Arab curse-vocabulary is extremely comprehensive and contains numerous gradations; but the supreme gradation is always the ancient Esperanto of the fist.

To many readers this observation will come as a surprise, for we love to talk about the necessity of the Jews in Palestine "establishing closer contact" with the natives, mixing with them, and so on, in order to make our peace with them. This may or may not be so. But I tell only of what I saw, and I saw that the closer we approached, the less hope there was of peace. And perhaps this could be observed not only in Palestine. That old wise man Mendelssohn, too, once thought that the Jews, by forcing themselves into the life of Germany, would attain brotherhood. Shall we discuss the consequences? Careful, my friends.

Chapter XV

Our Officers

I have promised to describe our men and officers. They made a "gathering of exiles." More than ten thousand men signed on in the Judean Regiments (the official name given us after the war), but about half of them I never saw – they were recruited too late. The war had ended meanwhile, and it was not worthwhile sending them to the front. They were demobilized direct from our base at Plymouth, where they had gone through their training under the command of the Jewish Colonel Miller, whom I also did not know.

In Palestine we had only about five thousand, distributed in three battalions: the Thirty-eighth, Thirty-ninth and Fortieth Royal Fusiliers, later known as the First, Second and Third Judean Battalions. I must say, however, that both the first and second names remained still-born. From G.H.Q. down to the Arab villages we were known (often even in official correspondence) as the "Jewish Regiment" – the very name which it had been desired to give us originally, and against which the assimilationists had made so bitter a protest to Lord Derby.

The English and the Americans were to be found in the Thirty-eighth and Thirty-ninth Battalions, though the former was more

"English" and the latter almost entirely "American." The Palestinians all served together, at first as the Fortieth Battalion, and later, when demobilization had forced the other two out of existence, as the First Judean Battalion.

The Thirty-eighth Battalion was led by Colonel Patterson, the Thirty-ninth by Colonel Margolin, and the Fortieth had a succession of three colonels – at first Samuel, then a Gentile, Scott, and finally Margolin.

Patterson was probably the only man in the British Army who entered the war as a lieutenant colonel and saw the war through without promotion and without having any order conferred upon him – though he served from beginning to end, and though both his Zion Mule Corps and his Jewish Battalion were several times mentioned in dispatches. Allenby, who promised him in writing that our battalion would be made a brigade and he would be its general, did not keep that promise. And after Patterson had taken up the cudgels several times on our behalf and sent strong protests against the official antisemitism which reigned in the army after the war, Allenby pettily revenged himself by not recommending him for promotion – nor any of our other colonels. Later, when I had become a member of the Zionist Executive, I wrote to Sir Herbert Samuel, appealing to him to consider Colonel Patterson when constituting his administration. I believe that Dr. Weizmann supported this request – but it was not granted.

The Jewish people also remained ungrateful to him. It is a painful subject to me, and one illustration will serve to characterize the complete attitude to him. At the Twelfth Congress, in Carlsbad in 1921, my appeal that he should be given a seat on the platform went unheeded, and the president of the Congress, in welcoming the guests, did not even mention his name.

But he remained the same true friend of the Jewish people and of Zionism. He did much for the Keren Hayesod in America, beloved of all who worked with him; and on those infrequent occasions when I still meet him in London or Paris, and I tell him of my disillusionments and troubles, he smiles with that same Irish smile as after our interview with the adjutant-general, or as at the close of weary, troubled days in Transjordan – a smile which made one forget generals, and malaria, and the enemy's guns, the smile of a man who believes in the ultimate triumph of inflexible determination. And he lifts his glass and says, "It will be all right in the end. The Jews are a great people. Here is to trouble." This is his favorite toast, for he believes that troubles are the essence of life, the mainspring of all progress.

I have already mentioned Margolin. By temperament it is he, not Patterson, who should have been an Englishman. The measure of his loquacity is ten words a day, and his thoughts are those of a man who spent his life away from the big cities – in Palestine in the days of the first pioneers, in the Australian bush – at the back of beyond, as they say in Australia: unhurried, earnest thoughts, monosyllabic and deep, marked throughout with a keen common sense. His American soldiers used to call him "Dad," although his punctiliousness often irritated them. As a matter of fact he did like to go into the most minute details of his soldiers' lives, like the "bonus paterfamilias" of Roman law. His camp was considered exemplary – so much so that English and Hindu battalions used to send their junior officers to learn orderliness and discipline. He believed in discipline unconditionally, and disapproved manifestly, though silently, of Patterson's seditiousness in combating the antisemites at Headquarters. But it was not due to timorousness toward Headquarters. In April, 1920, when members of the Jerusalem Hagana (self-defense) were being conveyed under escort to serve their terms of hard labor, he came to Lod with all his soldiers to shake hands with the "convicts"; and when, a year later, in May, 1921, Herbert Samuel appointed him chief of the Jewish half of that mixed Jewish-Arab militia which was one of Samuel's pet notions, Margolin did not ask for anybody's permission to bring his soldiers fully armed to Tel Aviv in the very midst of the Jaffa pogrom. For this misdeed he was forced to resign, and now he is back in Australia, longing for Palestine, where once he plowed the fields in Rehovot, fought in the Jordan Valley, ruled Es Salt in the land of Gilead.

Colonel Fred Samuel is a member of an Anglo-Jewish family which belongs to a long-assimilated milieu; into this circle, however, there came one personal force which strongly influenced many of those who belonged to it, and brought them back to the Jewish fold. I believe I have already mentioned Nina Davis. Today this name is, unfortunately, that of one of the departed. She was the wife of Dr. Redcliffe Salaman. Like Salaman and Samuel (who are related), Nina Davis came of a family established in England for generations, but her father, himself a man of whom much could be written, gave her a thorough Jewish education, and she grew up with a good knowledge and a deep love of the Hebrew language and literature. She wrote a number of books for Jewish children, stories and poems, as well as beautiful translations of Yehuda HaLevy, the Ibn Ezras and Gabirol. She had true literary talent, but her greatest gift was what people called "personal magnetism." She would have been, I have always thought, one of those intellectuals who in eighteenth-century France were the "salon queens"; and though, living away from London, she created no "salon," the influence she exercised was strong, nonetheless. The genuinely "English" group in English Zionism is very small, but its finest members are those who were attracted to it, directly or indirectly, by Nina Davis.

Among these was Colonel Samuel. At the beginning of the war he served in France, was already a lieutenant colonel in a well-known regiment, and doubtless had expectations of attaining a general's rank. At Dr. Salaman's call he left his battalion – no light or simple sacrifice for a commander – and came to take over our training camp, knowing well that this meant farewell to promotion, for the general of a Jewish brigade would naturally have been Patterson.

The greater part of his service in Palestine was with the Palestine volunteers. I was often struck by his tact and his wise flexibility. The whole spirit of his men was absolutely strange to him; his own psychological make-up was stiffly English, thoroughly imbued with English tradition, in which – both in civil and in military life – class is class, officer and man follow their own particular paths, the social scheme of things is unalterably fixed. Here he met simple soldiers, like Ben-Zvi or Ben-Gurion or Berl Katznelson, who, in another sense, themselves "commanded" larger numbers of men than could be found in a battalion; he found a "public opinion" in the battalion which he had to consider in order to avoid friction. There was a time when it was feared that he would not succeed in establishing between himself and the party leaders in uniform that relationship which could insure harmony and discipline. But he did succeed. His critics would complain that he introduced a Russian institution into the British Army – a battalion "soviet." His supporters could with justice retort that this "Russian" institution had an English model. Cromwell's army also had its soldiers' committee which the commanders would consult – with beneficial effects on discipline.

Colonel M. F. Scott is the embodiment of the Jewish idea of the "Righteous among the Gentiles." There could be found divided opinions about the other three commanders, but not about him. An elderly man, deeply religious, he believes in the Almighty, in the Gospels and in the Old Testament. He is a man not of our times. His religious conception is that Jesus Christ only brought the promise of world redemption; the fulfillment of the promise will come with the redemption of God's chosen people.

Scott is a Christian through and through, and believes that Christianity will be the ultimate religion of humanity. But he is not a "missionary." Nobody has the right to interfere with the belief of Israel; it is a duty only to help Israel establish its Home. For then the Eternal People will again become a People of Priests and will bring peace to the religious conscience of the world. It is an honor and a privilege for England to assist in hastening the consummation of the Divine purpose. And every son of England called to take his part in this work must approach it and fulfill it with awe and veneration.

For a long time Scott was the commander of the Palestine volunteers. But he adopted a method entirely different from Samuel's.

Knowing that he was a stranger, he made it his business not to influence the inner life of his battalion; he accepted it as he found it, contenting himself with the role of guardian, protecting his men from any clash with the varied elements in the army about them. For one particular action he deserves the gratitude of the whole Jewish people. At the close of summer in 1919, he was suddenly ordered to send eighty of his men to Egypt. Who it was that conceived this order, and why it was issued, remained a well-kept secret. But the order was unjust, for we had from the beginning been assured that Jewish soldiers would be called on to serve only in Palestine. The battalion as one man declared that the eighty men would not go. It was the colonel's disciplinary duty to arrest the eighty and to appeal for military assistance against the rest of the battalion. Had he done so, the consequences would have been most unpleasant. But Scott handled the matter wonderfully, and risked facing a court-martial. He arrested nobody, and informed Headquarters that the order was regarded by his battalion as unjust and, what was more, as an attempt to incite the Arabs, for the latter would feel that Palestine Jews were fighting against Egyptian Nationalists. The eighty men could not be blamed, for the whole battalion had declared its intention of not allowing them to go. The only action he could therefore take was to arrest the whole battalion, which meant trying the best young men in the Yishuv. He did not consider himself justified in taking such a step, and he therefore respectfully suggested that Headquarters should consider the matter, and rather consult London. And he added that the service of the men was excellent, discipline above reproach, and all orders obeyed with absolute precision. Every day he dispatched the same report to Headquarters: discipline irreproachable, service first class, but will not hear of sending eighty men to Egypt. Headquarters was compelled to forward his reports to London, and within a couple of weeks a reply came from the War Office to the effect that the battalion should be left in peace, and that the whole incident should be consigned to oblivion.

Today, Scott lives in a little town near London. On the infrequent occasions when the ex-Legionaries come together in commemoration of the Legion, he comes along and says, "I am happy that God granted me the privilege of serving in Palestine with Jewish soldiers." And every evening, together with his wife and two children, he offers a prayer for the redemption of Israel in its own country, as the beginning of the redemption of the world.

Once, on a Zionist Congress, I repeated a sentence of his. It is worth mentioning here also: "It was England's privilege to accept the greatest of honors: we tore out of the Bible the page bearing the most ancient of prophecies – and we endorsed the Lord's own pledge. No nation can repudiate such a signature."

There are many such Englishmen, and they are the true England. Though not all of them may say these prayers aloud, Scott's soul is the soul of England. This we dare never forget, however bitter our justified criticism may be.

Our other officers deserve mention. In Patterson's battalion two-thirds of them were Jews; in the other two the majority were Gentiles.

Apparently, the agitation against the Legion carried on by the assimilationists had its full effect in that section of Anglo-Jewry from which most of the Jewish officers in the British Army were drawn. As long as Dr. Redcliffe Salaman was in London, his personal influence brought over to us a fair number of officers, but with his departure for Palestine, only such as were moved by a natural urge came to us – that is, very few.

Several of these "spontaneous" phenomena were interesting. In the early days after the official creation of the Legion, a very young Guardsman, second lieutenant in one of the oldest Guards regiments, paid a visit to our office. His name was Harold Rubin, and he was the son of a wealthy pearl merchant. He told us his story, of which I remember but one fact – that he was educated at Eton.

His home upbringing was far removed from the influence of Judaism, even from religious customs. The explanation he gave for his coming to us was a simple one. He saw in a newspaper that a Jewish regiment was being formed, and decided there and then that that was his place. Anybody who knows what Eton and a Guards regiment mean to a wealthy English Jew will appreciate the emphasis with which I mention this case. It was an exception, though optimists may consider it a sign of the times.

A similar exception was provided by Lieutenant Edwin Samuel, a son of Sir Herbert, who was then beloved of the Palestinians.

A small portion of our Jewish officers settled in Palestine after the war: Horace Samuel, who became a leading barrister in Jerusalem; Israel Jaffe, from Belfast, the possessor of three university degrees, who played an unsuspected though important role at a critical time for the Yishuv, and who will yet, I am certain, become a great figure in Palestine; Jacobs, who became the secretary of the Zionist Executive in Jerusalem, and several others. Among those who did not remain in Palestine can be counted a number of active Zionists. The majority came and went, served honorably and worthily, but remained unmoved by either the glamour of Zionism or the magic of Palestine.

Closely observing these men, I found a new confirmation of an old conviction: that it is not true that Palestine converts one to Zionism. It only happens with those who previously had, perhaps even unknown to themselves, that element in their blood which we call Zionism. For Zionism is a peculiar characteristic of the soul, similar to what among other people and in other circumstances gives birth to the "outposts of empire pioneers," to men whom we call adventurers – men who refuse to accept a ready-made ladder of life on which to climb, but must create a new ladder themselves. The day will come when the whole Jewish people will make its peace with Zionism, perhaps even lend Zionism its support. But even then there will be only a small minority of "Zionists." A Zionist must be born.

Among our Gentile colleagues we had several enthusiastic sympathizers, like the Welsh Major Hopkin (now Labor MP), deeply respected by the Palestinians. But the majority of them were just like the majority of Jewish officers, faithful, correct and neutral. Whether there were any undisclosed antisemites among them, I do not know. One must be careful with the word "antisemite." We need not blind ourselves. We ourselves are often troubled by some of the characteristics we have inherited from the ghetto. But when a Gentile permits himself to notice them we call him antisemite; and, worse, when he says nothing we feel certain that he thinks like one. I have never been interested in this probing into Gentile hearts, perhaps because I have not been blessed with such an interest in my neighbors, Gentile or Jewish, as to make me immerse myself in their unexpressed thoughts.

There was one officer who openly hated us, though I should hesitate to call even him an antisemite. It was a certain Major Smolley, Margolin's second-in-command. Our American boys suffered much at his hands, and on one occasion his tactlessness brought about a great misfortune, to which I shall refer. But I met this very man under other circumstances, and was given an entirely different impression. I am certain that had he been just an official in the War Office, and given the affairs of the Jewish battalions to handle, he would have treated us in the friendliest manner possible. But coming into daily contact with a psychology absolutely strange to his own, he could not find the right attitude to adopt. It is precisely this that is the trouble with many of the British officials in Palestine today.

Chapter XVI

Our Soldiers

Our men may be easily divided into three groups: the English, the Palestinians and the Americans.

I have already said much about the English boys. I have told how the name "tailors," at first almost a curse word, gradually became an honorable name. Without a doubt they demonstrated that they were among the best soldiers in the British Army. Inspired by nothing, loving nothing except their homes, their wives and their children somewhere in Whitechapel or Leeds, indifferent to Zionism, indifferent to Palestine, angry with a world that had disturbed their peace and dragged them across the ocean to fight for something in which they were not interested – they performed their new tasks conscientiously from A to Z, from polishing their buttons to exercising with bayonets, to shooting at the Turk in the darkness of Jordan Valley nights, to giving up their lives like heroes. Our battalions passed through difficult moments, outbursts of collective impatience which several times endangered the very existence of the Legion, but never were the "tailors" affected. To them, everything – danger, heat, rudeness, the interminable monotony of peace service, sleeping on rocks, keeping guard on lonely hills, malaria, a wound, an empty water-flask – everything was part of the "job" which had been undertaken and must be done conscientiously to the end, with just a little grumbling. Grumbling, they say, is the soldier's only privilege, and even Napoleon called his best men "the old grumblers." Eternally discontented, yet eternally true to duty.

I saw nothing of any collective life among them. They had no common interests, held no meetings, displayed no tendencies to any kind of unification. There existed lonely little groups – often accidental groups, determined by the apportionment of tents made by a sergeant who had no concern with the existence of friendships or relationships. "These tent-companions will be your new friends." They gave each other what assistance they could, played cards together, gossiped about their work or told home reminiscences. No sign of longing for the friends of yesterday's tent. Longing was reserved for only one thing – "home."

They hated the war as the brutal lunacy of a drunken world which was not and could not be justified; they regarded the Palestine volunteers simply as fools. And yet, when the Russians had signed the treaty of Brest-Litovsk, and G.H.Q., with an eye to breaking up the Legion, ordered Patterson to give them, as "Russians," the option of transferring to a labor battalion, and Patterson paraded them at Helmieh, telling them that they could freely go to a labor battalion far from the front and from danger, of the thousand and more on the parade ground only two left the battalion.

Nor could I say why they proved to be the best boxers in the whole British Army in Palestine, defeating, one after another, the champions of all other regiments, so that in the final match in Cairo between "England" and "Australia," it was our soldier Burak who represented England.

Palestine just did not interest them. After the Armistice they were told that they would be given an opportunity to visit all the historic spots in the country at the expense of the army. Only a very small number utilized the opportunity; the majority chose rather to remain in the camp guarding empty magazines or Turkish prisoners. One of them sent Colonel Patterson an anonymous letter, respectfully couched in the following terms: "We do not need this. We did not come here on a visit. We came to serve in the war, have served well and have always been true to you, sir, in every trouble and danger. Now you should be true to us. The war is ended. Help us to return home as soon as possible...." And they applauded vociferously when a singer at one of the concerts composed new words about "home" to a popular army tune.

Yet, though they were longing with all their hearts for demobilization, this did not lessen by one iota the punctilious fulfillment of their duties. There was not a sign among them of that weariness, that negligence, that degeneration of discipline, which was so painfully noticeable at that time in every English battalion. Perhaps this was why they were among the last to be demobilized.

And thus the summary of their record: the first to arrive, the last to depart; strangers in their coming, strangers at their going; throughout their service –quiet, correct and punctilious in camp, quiet, unflinching and brave under fire. An altogether curious psychology, one to which I am not sympathetic; yet I cannot and do not wish to deny that there is in it something of a peculiar wholeness and greatness.

When I wrote "the last to depart," I was referring only to those who came from overseas. I did not take into account the Palestine volunteers. The final remnant of the Legion, which was demobilized only in 1921 after the Jaffa pogrom, consisted of the Palestine volunteers.

Of them, Weizmann said to Allenby, "Garibaldi did not have better men" – and he was right. Of the innumerable blunders committed by Allenby in Palestine, I hold his attitude to the volunteers to have been one of the worst. He would not, or did not know how to utilize the first-class military material which at least three-quarters of them represented. Their bravery was on a par with that which roused the imagination of the Jewish world in the defenders of Tel Hai: men who stand fast, fifty against five thousand, men who are not only not afraid but who long for self-sacrifice, dreaming of death as a sacred purpose. And men – many of them – of a high order of intelligence, highly-educated, courteous, chivalrous in their conception of honor, camaraderie and duty. Moreover, men who, many of them, knew Palestine as they knew the fingers of their own hands; nearly all of them spoke Arabic, many as well as the Arabs themselves; some had served in the Turkish army; many were expert shots and horsemen. One had to be blind or surrounded by blind counselors in order to obstruct – as Allenby did with so much success – the utilization of such recruits.

One incident illustrates the spirit which fired them. A number of them proposed, through their colonel, that they should be permitted to undertake the task, regarded universally as at once the most dangerous and the most deserving of honor, of stealing through the enemy lines, toward Samaria and Galilee, in order to determine the true position in the Turkish camp and even to agitate among the men in that camp. In nine cases out of ten this would have meant certain death, for every one of them was well known in the enemy camp. Many parents awaited in trembling the receipt of Headquarters' reply. The reply was "No" – though I do not believe for a moment that this decision was prompted by any concern for their young lives.

There was much delay in bringing them from their training camp at Tel El Kebir in Egypt to Palestine. The Yishuv decided to take the initiative. Mrs. Grosovsky, of Tel Aviv, led the attack. She was the wife of a man who once sat, impoverished and hungry, together with young Eliezer ben Yehuda in a cold Paris loft, where they decided that Hebrew must again become a living tongue and must be spoken with the Sephardic pronunciation – that type of "madman." It is told that when Grosovsky built his house he buried several bottles of Carmel wine in the garden and swore that none of it would be touched until one of two things happened: the entry of one of his children into a Hebrew University or into a Jewish Army.... Mrs. Grosovsky had two sons in the Legion. She organized a deputation of women, mothers of the men, who traveled to G.H.Q. to interview the commander-in-chief himself.

"We are hearing all kinds of rumors in the country," she told him, "and our children are far away from us. We don't feel safe." I have remarked before that this man, with his "Bull of Bashan" reputation, was in reality painfully weak. The real difficulty one had was in finding an approach to him, but once this was achieved and one could talk to him, he was the most easily influenced of men. Several weeks later the Palestine battalion was stationed at Sarafend, near Lod and Jaffa.

The internal life of their battalion was most "highbrow." It was a delight to see their camp library with its five thousand books in several languages. Through the meetings they held in camp they conducted the whole Labor Movement in the country and sent delegates to the Provisional Council (now the National Council) of the Jewish Community. A postal official once told me that there were days when a few privates in the Fortieth Battalion, Royal Fusiliers, received more letters than the whole of the General Staff. When the Zionist Commission considered important matters – like a new colonization scheme in the South, which was mooted at the time, or the question of a constitution for Palestine – the opinion of the Fortieth Battalion was among the first asked. And they remained good soldiers. "Punctilious in duty," Colonel Scott had said, even under such conditions as would be classed as mutiny in military regulations.

I thought the finest among them to be the former Jaffa College students. The "Herzlia Gymnasium" was often criticized both from the religious traditional point of view because of its mixed classes, as well as from the purely pedagogic point of view. But whatever the merits of these complaints, I must say emphatically that the Herzlia did train "character" – in those days, at any rate. In some of the Herzlia students, more than in any other group, I found intelligence, reserve, courtesy, respect for achievements, chivalry, and an inspired preparedness for self-sacrifice. I can only wish this "mother" of Hebrew higher education that her future "generations," as well as her many daughter-schools in Palestine and Europe, should possess in a like degree these moral and national virtues.

In order to deal justly with the various groups among the Palestine volunteers it would be necessary to write a book. The Sephardim require a book to themselves: young men from the border of East and West, refreshingly clear-cut in all their feeling. Their attitude to Palestine and Zionism and their attitude to the Arab neighbors (hardly an enthusiastic one, to put it mildly) were not matters of opinion or for discussion, but were naturally instinctive; they are perhaps the only element among the Jews which does not suffer from overcleverness, from distorted vision, an element which uses its eyes and not tinted spectacles and has the direct normal intelligence, the simple, clear faculty of comprehension of all normal peoples.

Or the Turkish prisoners, Jews from Smyrna and Constantinople, who had been living undisturbed and well-fed in the prison camp at Sidi Bishr by Alexandria, but suddenly demanded that they should be permitted to fight for the Jewish National Home.

Or the Yemenites, probably the most talented Jews in the whole world, wonderfully gifted intellectually, in music and in commerce – quite a separate "people," with its own physical characteristics, whose origin is a mystery of the dim past, and who, in the face of endless generations of the most terrible brutal slavery, kept alive within itself a brilliant spark of learning; young men whose parents had arrived in Palestine emaciated and bare, carrying their all in two tins; young men who refused to eat meat throughout the whole period of their service – for the kosher regulations which Patterson had so strenuously fought for and so stringently enforced at Portsmouth, had, under front conditions, long become a dead letter.

The Palestine volunteers remained the final bearers of the Legion idea; fought tooth and nail against demobilization; held the rifle until it was virtually dragged from their hands. It was not an easy matter for them. Their service began with a profound disillusionment: the offensive and the victory came in September, 1918, while they were still in training. Then came peace and from all sides they heard of new projected constructive activities. The word *kevutza* was becoming a sacred password – and they, former workers, inspired by the ideal of labor, were compelled to guard the railway at Haifa or the aqueduct at Rafah on the fringe of the Sinai Desert. It was inordinately difficult to endure. Many did not. But several hundred clung stubbornly to the belief that upbuilding work could be assured only by defense, that the Yishuv without the Legion would be like a village of wooden huts without a fire extinguisher, and they set themselves determinedly against demobilization. They contrived to have their period of engagement extended for three months (G.H.Q. would not permit a longer extension), and then for a further three months. Then they enlisted in Herbert Samuel's mixed militia, though they, in common with the whole Yishuv, were against the project – until the Jaffa pogrom put an end both to Samuel's militia and to their military service.

The Americans presented a complex problem. In number they constituted the major group in the Legion. They were of a high order of intelligence, of bravery and of physical development. But their psychology found it very difficult to suit itself to the conditions in Palestine; not because of their Jewish, but because of their American characteristics.

There is a wide gulf separating the English mentality from that of the Jew. Yet this gulf is as nothing to the abyss which separates the English psychology from the American. I have lived among Russians, Italians, Germans, Frenchmen and Turks; never have I seen two peoples so different in character as the English and the American. Many thinkers in both countries are well aware of this; I cannot forget something I was once told by the erudite editor of an English newspaper, who was himself anxious to promote Anglo-American friendship. "It is fortunate," he said, "that we live so far from one another. Had we been neighbors, the world would have witnessed for the first time a demonstration of what national hatred really means." But the rest of the world is unaware of this. One hears the same language, the same names, and one believes that here are kindred spirits. Kindred spirits! In our own miniature world, in the Legion, I was afforded clear proof of this "kinship." Our men were, of course, only half American; but even this partial "Americanization" was sufficient to render the English atmosphere intolerable for them. It was far easier for the Russians, the Sephardim or the Yemenites to accustom themselves to English ways than for these young men who for ten or fifteen years had breathed the air of the United States.

In what the difference consists, is a subject for a book. I do not intend to write that book but desire to emphasize only one important contrast: the contrast of tempo. The American thinks quickly, makes an immediate decision and sets about carrying it out. The Englishman, on the other hand, can do this only in moments of extreme danger. Even then his "speed" is purely relative. Under more or less normal circumstances the Englishman is closely related to the Spaniard with his *mañana* and the Arab with his *bukra*. Both mean the same: "Tomorrow!" "Don't stampede me! What's the hurry? Let's put it off, sleep on it, for a week, a month, a year, sometime."

Then the American is strictly practical: before he considers something, he first of all wants to know what the end, the result will be; and whatever he does today must be suited to the needs of that future result. The Englishman does not like this conception of doing things. He is proud of his unconcern for the possibilities of next year; of all the Hebrew proverbs he has translated, it is "sufficient unto the day is the evil thereof" that he loves best. Snow and fire are more closely related than this public school psychology and the soul of a Chicago "hustler." I have no desire to judge which is the better of the two. But they are hardly conducive to harmony.

In our theater this contrast was clearly and incisively reflected. American young men, on leaving the boat at Alexandria, instantly wanted to know, "Where is the front?" The Englishman replied, "First do your training." The American retorted, "But in your country's camps they tell you that three or four months' training is quite enough – and we've had six." The Englishman's reply was, "We'll see about that in God's good time." With the result that most of them missed the offensive – the purpose for which they had come.

Then came peace, and there was talk of upbuilding the country. Most of the Americans were good Zionists. Again they asked the American question: "Well, if there's no war, there's at least upbuilding. Where is the upbuilding? Send us to the plows." But the Spaniard in British uniform answered, "*Mañana.*"

I am far from wishing to blame one side. I blame both. For the ex-legionaries in New York, Toronto and everywhere else I have the highest regard; but they are intelligent men and would hardly wish me simply to hand them bouquets. I blame both sides – and the Jews more than the others. It was their national duty not to allow even *mañana* and *bukra* to paralyze them. This, however, was the error they committed. When they saw that the war was over and that the upbuilding of the country was still in the mists of "tomorrow," many of them decided that there was no purpose in just wearing khaki, and began to demand demobilization.

In the summer of 1919, representatives of the American and Palestinian men, together with workers' spokesmen, held a big meeting at Petah Tikva. (If I am not mistaken, it was at that conference that was established the "Ahdut ha-Avoda," which is now the most important labor party in Palestine.) I attended, and I warned them gravely that the most important period of the Legion's existence was just beginning; a gigantic campaign of pogrom-propaganda was being carried on, and could, moreover, depend on sympathy in military circles of varying degrees of importance. Our enemies were firmly convinced that neither the British nor the Indian troops would lift a finger to protect the Yishuv; in their street demonstrations they were shouting, "The Government is with us!" Whether they were right or not was not of immediate importance: they believed it. But there was one force of which they were afraid: the Jewish Legion. This was the factor which was preventing even the unrest in Egypt from finding reflected expression in Palestine; for the enemy knew that there were still five thousand Jewish soldiers in the country. How dare we speak of demobilization?

It availed little. True, the blame did not lie only with the legionaries. Had they been convinced, as I was, that there was danger lurking, they would themselves have demanded to be retained. Of this I am certain. But there were people in the Yishuv who "reassured" them. They were told that the man who had been warning them of danger was himself a newcomer to the country and knew nothing of the true position; they, the "reassurers," however, were local inhabitants; they knew the Arab and were emphatically positive that he would never make a pogrom – this was ten months before the pogrom in Jerusalem! But for the Americans this was naturally a powerful argument. Who talks of the danger? An "outlander." Who says, "We need no forces"? The men on the spot. Consequently...

Consequently there was trouble. It is not pleasant to relate the details. The result was that many who had been among the last arrivals were the first to leave. Within a short while, after the meeting at Petah Tikva, only two of our three battalions remained, then only one – the Palestine volunteers – and then only a part of that. In the spring of 1919 we had five thousand men: one year later we had but three to four hundred. Then came the catastrophe in Jerusalem, the Passover pogrom of 1920....

Chapter XVII

The Caste of the General Staff

The Jerusalem pogrom was the inevitable outcome of the attitude and tactics of Allenby's staff. It happened that these tactics could be directed against a helpless victim – the Legion – which, because it was under military command, could be attacked and bullied with impunity. But this was only a detail. The decrees from which the Legion suffered were directed not only against the Legion but against the whole Yishuv, and worse – against Zionism.

Just how and why such an attitude existed at G.H.Q. is another story. The result of it was that atmosphere which we ordinarily call antisemitism, which is how I shall describe it. But in speaking of the causes, I repeat – do not take the word "antisemitism" too literally. Neither Allenby nor even Bols was a Jew-hater; of the others I shall mention there was perhaps only one who could be so described – Colonel Gabriel. But not Lawrence, nor Philby, nor even Ronald Storrs, to whom an unkind Italian observer, Commandant Levi-Bianchini, always referred as Don Rinaldo Orientale – were antisemites. One or two of them may even once have had a cold regard for Zionism.

What was it, then, that made them all antisemitic agitators and brought one of them – General Bols, the Military Administrator of Occupied Territory – to play the part, on a smaller scale, of a Plehve?

To understand this, we must return for a moment to consider those characteristics of the English of which I have so often spoken. The average Englishman of the ruling caste is inherently opposed to any big, far-reaching project, and at least he is averse to expressing sympathy with such projects. He considers it bad form. More so when any scheme smacks of sentimentalism, of repairing the world's ills, of saving somebody or other from Lord knows what. And worse still, when such a scheme has a romantic flavor about it, he feels that these things are suitable for intellectual dilettantes, not for serious-minded, conservative gentlemen. It is worst of all when the execution of such a scheme falls on the shoulders of England itself.

Not all England is thus; not even the majority. I speak of the ruling caste. And even here there are hundreds of exceptions, dreamers like Balfour, like Amery, like Graham or Ormsby-Gore or Kenworthy, Steed or Wedgwood, and many, many others. But that "caste," those half-million souls who are connected with or related to the peerage, who all go to the ancient public schools at Eton, Harrow, Winchester, and then study not just at Oxford or Cambridge, but at distinguished colleges like Balliol or Christchurch, which are eight hundred years old – that caste is a world of its own, distinct from the rest of English humanity, deaf and proud of its deafness, unimaginative and proud of it. Do you want an exact parallel to their outlook? Take the old ghetto. Other days, other customs, but the same fanaticism of "We are chosen," the very same disregard for the world outside, "Pooh!" to everything new. Fortunately, the time is long past when this ruling caste really conducted the affairs of state. Today the decisive role is played by other, broader and more vital elements; in the ministries, even in the bureaucratic offices, there are many men of an altogether different mentality. But the practical execution of decisions still lies largely in the hands of this "caste."

It is the army, however, in which it is most strongly represented, and the higher the rank the stronger. This requires no explanation – for everybody knows it as a fact. Kitchener, with his antagonism to "fancy" regiments, was a typical example. They are antagonistic in exactly the same way to everything tinged with "fancy," to anything that is not quite twice-two – for instance, an offensive on the Eastern front; for instance, Zionism.

Now imagine a military clique – a "caste" within a "caste" – in the heat of war, on the Palestine front. Suddenly they receive an order, like a bolt from the blue: support Zionism. We are sending you a Jewish Legion. We are sending you a Zionist Commission. Their first plaint is: Were we asked about it before you made your decision in London? No, we were not asked. And even a civil servant in peacetime does not like this. The second plaint is: This is politics and, moreover, politics of a kind most unpopular with the population of the very land you have asked us to "liberate." Can't you understand that politics, especially of this kind, will hinder, not help, our campaign? Couldn't you wait until the end of the war, when our job would be finished, before carrying out your schemes?

I admit that even to me these complaints sound almost convincing. To them they were unanswerable. And then, consider the cause of these complaints – in itself in crying disharmony to the whole tradition and outlook of the "caste"!

Yet this was only half the trouble. The other half was probably just as important. Here I come to the names I mentioned earlier – Lawrence and Philby. I limit myself to these two, but there are many others – for even the caste has its own dreamers. They chose an idea which was in complete harmony with the most honored English traditions – not wild, not novel, not "fancy." Their dream was "Greater Arabia." England has administered countries where Arabic is spoken, like Egypt or the Sudan, for over forty years. There is a mountain of accumulated experience for dealing with such peoples. They would be "liberated," they would be united and they would be called "Greater Arabia." They would even be given Arab kings, picturesque sheiks in green turbans, dear grown-up children who sit on divans with their legs crossed under them and who require English advisers in all matters of state. Such a dream – rather!

The English bureaucracy in Egypt before the war consisted almost entirely of such Arabophiles. That was the reason they had elected to join the Civil Service in Egypt – not an easy undertaking, for it required a knowledge of Arabic. With the outbreak of war, they donned khaki and created the "background" for Military Headquarters. Lawrence and Philby were thus only representative of their class – which counted its scores, all of them born members of the "caste."

Colonel Lawrence himself was an extremely interesting man. Long before the first offensive in the Sinai Desert, clad in Arab garments and in daily danger of his life, he visited the important points in the Arab peninsula, broadcasting the message of a "Greater Arabia" which England wished to give them. Philby later did the same in the depths of the least-known portion of the peninsula – Nedjd, the land of the Wahabites, where he attempted to persuade Sultan Ibn Saud to make his peace with other Arab rulers and to fight together for a Greater Arabia. The narrative of their experiences reads like a romance; but it is hardly relevant here. What I wish to emphasize is the essential element of their common dream: the "Greater Arabia" must unconditionally remain "picturesque"; camels, caravans, white burnooses, green turbans, veiled women, harems – the full decoration of the Orient must be religiously retained. They shudder at the thought that this beauty may be disturbed by an overdose of civilization. It may be that behind it all there lies the instinctive feeling that only so long as the king sits on the ground with his legs crossed under him will he require English advisers. However this may be, the desire to eternalize the palm-decorations rings out from every line they wrote; and this desire, too, is typical of their whole class. Did not Storrs write: "As long as I live I shall not allow tramways in Jerusalem"? Another of the same school, Stephen Graham, who "discovered" Russia, would sing hymns of praise in his books to the Russian autocracy and to the justice of banishment to Siberia as a punishment; and after the Kerensky Revolution he wrote in the *Times* that he was bitterly grieved; that he had hoped that Russia would forever remain a kind of museum of medieval customs.

The Balfour Declaration stabbed these Lawrences and Philbys to the heart. They had seen Jews, both rich – in Lady N. N.'s salon – and poor, in Whitechapel – quite sufficient for them to realize that the idea of the National Home had nothing to do with "picturesque" Hasidim with curls (which they could certainly have "swallowed," for they are not Jew-haters), but with modern Jews, wearing trousers on their legs and hats on their heads, and with European ideas under those hats. An end to all the *couleur locale*! Tramcars in Jerusalem! instead of camels and palms, red roofs of brand new colonies, where girls and young men would walk freely together, just as in England! Horrors!

This is not a joke. It is the absolute truth. Lawrence published an article in a London newspaper at the time, in which, despite himself, one could hear the echo of gnashing teeth. He was for Zionism, he wrote, but only on one condition: that the Jews must not go to Palestine as Europeans or Americans. They must suit themselves to the Arab customs of living – "Orientalize" themselves. Otherwise, they would ruin both themselves and the country.

None of this is antisemitism. But the consequence of these influences was an unprecedented epidemic of antisemitism. I repeat: unprecedented. Not in Russia, nor in Poland had there been seen such an intense and widespread atmosphere of hatred as prevailed in the British Army in Palestine in 1919 and 1920. Even "tradition" was overlooked in the ecstasy of excitement. It is tradition that politics are barred in officers' clubs, and particularly criticism of the government. Yet in the clubs of Allenby's officers, from G.H.Q. down to guards over Turkish prisoners, the Jews were enthusiastically cursed and the "silly" Balfour Declaration roundly condemned. From the officers the epidemic soon spread to the sergeants, and then to privates in every tent. In the Indian regiments, men born in the Punjab or in the Himalayas would, in their own language, discuss the same topic – their own English officers told me so.

Perhaps a quotation from one document will be sufficient to illustrate the spirit in which the army was "trained." Shortly before the Jerusalem pogrom every battalion received a circular, which was to be read out not only to officers but to sergeants as well. I still have a copy of the document, which opens as follows:

"As the Government had to pursue in Palestine a policy unpopular with the majority of the population, trouble may be expected to arise...."

On the Mount of Olives, the seat of the Occupied Enemy Territory Administration, they began to come out into the open. The chief administrator in 1919 was General Money, but the real dominating figure was Vivian Gabriel. He wore a colonel's uniform, was head of the finance department and pulled all the strings in the government. He was not a pure Englishman: it was said that one of his parents was Maltese. (The population of the island of Malta is of Arab origin, speaks an Arabic dialect, which is written in Latin characters, and is fanatically Catholic.) Perhaps this was the origin of his hatred for the Jews – an Arab and Catholic combination. For I regard him, without any modification whatever, as a true enemy of the Jews. He was, moreover, perhaps the only member of the administration possessed of real ability: acute, educated, and with a thorough knowledge of the economic and political conditions of the country.

He knew Zionism, or at least knew our weak points: he knew the faults of our agricultural system, he knew of the friction between the old orthodoxy and the new immigrants, of the failings of the Zionist Commission's financial system. He openly declared himself to be an anti-Zionist and openly hindered us at every step. To enumerate all his "good deeds" would be tiresome. Enough that these deeds distinguished themselves by their intensity and by an outstanding wealth of originality. A blow on every side. Today an order that all tax forms must be completed in English or Arabic – no other languages being valid; tomorrow a printed report to the London Government showing statistically that in the first place Palestine could subsist only on agriculture, and in the second that the Jews were a negligible factor in the agriculture of the country; the day after, an officially proclaimed scheme for settling thirty thousand Maltese immigrants on state lands.

General Money obeyed him as a child obeys its teacher. It was under Gabriel's influence that Money permitted himself to indulge publicly in an anti-Zionist manifestation. "*Hatikva*" had been recognized as our national anthem, for which all had to stand. General Wyndham, the High Commissioner of Egypt, had stood at the salute in Cairo for the singing of all the verses – quite a long time, incidentally. Allenby himself, at the laying of the foundation-stone of the Hebrew University, stood up for "*Hatikva*." General Money, at a Jewish meeting in a Jewish institution, in the presence of foreign representatives, remained seated.

Even fresh arrivals, newcomers from Egypt, would arrive poisoned against us. I remember one in particular – a newly-appointed governor for Jaffa. He arrived in the evening, immediately summoned a Jewish secretary and informed him that the next morning he would receive a Jewish deputation of welcome and would address them in Arabic. He was not an antisemite, he explained, and was very sympathetically disposed toward those Jews who were born in the country and spoke Arabic; but the others, the newcomers, really had no right to be in the country at all. The secretary immediately reported to the Zionist Commission. We telephoned General Money and told him that there would be trouble. The deputation would simply turn their backs on him and leave him in the middle of his Arabic speech. Even Money thought this undesirable, and the governor was told that he had better talk English and not talk too much. But he could not restrain himself for long. A month later, in a club, in the presence of a number of English officers and two French, he delivered himself as follows: "If they beat Jews here I shall open my window and watch; and I shall order the militia not to interfere." The two French officers were Jews – Dr. Jacques Segal and another. They reported to the Zionist Commission.

But clever as Gabriel was, there was one thing he did not understand: that it was only in Palestine that the Jews were weak; that elsewhere they had power – more power than, for instance, a group of officers on the Mount of Olives. By the end of 1919, both General Money and Colonel Gabriel had vanished from the scene. It was said in Palestine that this had been achieved by Mr. Brandeis, who, after a visit to Palestine, had gone to London and made an emphatic protest. Gabriel was most unhappy at having to leave the Mount of Olives. For a long time he continued to pursue the Maltese immigrants' scheme. But he failed, and consoled himself by writing anti-Zionist articles in London.

It is worth noting that Mr. Philby has had recourse to the same consolation. He has had other troubles compelling him to seek solace. His life's ambition was almost realized: he was sent as English adviser to a portion of his Arab Paradise – Transjordan. He stayed there for a year, observing Abdullah's system of government – and then left the country, disillusioned and embittered. It is remarkable that other protagonists of the perpetuation of the caravan and the harem have turned away from their ideal. Lawrence is silent. Richmond (who was later to Sir Herbert Samuel's administration what Gabriel had been to Money) is also silent; and Philby vents his spleen on the Jews and Zionism.

But the change in the O.E.T.A. availed us little. Instead of Money we had Bols – and the bloody Passover of 1920 in Jerusalem, three days of slaughter in the Holy City, the epopoeia of the self-defense, the military tribunal, the incarceration of the Jewish "criminals" in the fortress of Acre. All very "picturesque" – but not of my story. I write of the Legion – and the Legion was then no more. Had it only been …

It was but natural that the Jewish Regiment should become the cherished victim of this attitude. In order to make the life of the civil population unbearable, ingenuity was essential, and it was necessary to utilize the outstanding capabilities of a Gabriel; but to do the same to an ordinary soldier, it was enough to be just a corporal in the military police. A veritable hunt began….

I shall not give a detailed narrative – perhaps because of sentiment. For I wore British uniform for thirty months and am proud of it, and I am loath to discuss before strangers ugly petty details of a great and beautiful venture. I may criticize or even ridicule a General Allenby for his clumsy excursions into politics and civil administration, but Allenby the soldier is a different man for me, a great military leader, "Lord of Megiddo in the Valley of Esdraelon," the conqueror of Jerusalem and Gaza, of Galilee and Transjordan. May gods and men forgive him for the counselors with whom he barricaded himself and for the venom with which they poisoned one part of the great and noble family which is called the British Army. In spite of everything, it was my family, too; it is better not to tell.

My readers among the American and Canadian legionaries will also forgive me for not dealing with the two courts-martial, which sentenced fifty-four and then thirty-five of our American boys for mutiny. I, a lawyer by diploma, but a lawyer who had never appeared in a court of law, was called to defend them. It was a dark moment. But on this, too, I do not wish to dwell. Our men lived for months in an atmosphere of continual provocation from outside; and in the second of these unhappy cases, there was also provocation from within – from their own commander, the Major Smolley to whom I have referred. But when one is on guard at a time of danger – which was our task in Palestine – one dare not be trapped by provocation. I do not blame. As the trials proceeded I was drawn to these young men who bore themselves so honorably before the court; and one of them, Corporal Levinsky from Canada, acted in a superbly noble manner – he took all the blame on himself, declaring that he had forced his comrades to leave the camp. He was sentenced to seven years' military imprisonment and thereby saved six of his comrades. They were all amnestied four months later. And I shall never forget how, on their way back to Palestine, they came up to the fence of the same prison camp in Kantara where we had many times conferred during the trial, and where it was now I, with twenty others, who was the prisoner, and with trembling voices said, "Sir, it breaks our hearts to see you here…" I shall not forget it. Far be it from me to blame them: they are too dear to me. But dear, too, is the Legion idea. And there was a time when I had hoped that we would all of us just clench our teeth, shut our eyes and hold on, hold on…

I do not wish to create the impression that all in Allenby's Headquarters were our enemies, or that the enemies were only Christians and Arabs. On the contrary, the man who gave the hardest blow to the military clique and conclusively freed Palestine from its domination was one of the most important members of the Military Administration: Colonel Meinertzhagen, General Bols' political secretary. He told both Bols and Allenby frankly that the administration had erred badly. Despite all appeals, promises and threats, he forwarded a scathing report to the War Office and saw to it that it should be shown to Lloyd George and his cabinet. This was the real sledgehammer blow which finally smashed the control of the generals in Palestine.

And on the other hand there was not absent that personage, without whom, in our Exile tradition, no well-managed anti-Jewish campaign can get along: the Jewish informer. I shall not mention his name, but he is still to be seen in Anglo-Jewish London society. At that time he was a captain, talked of joining the Legion, but finally came to rest near the seats of the mighty G.H.Q.

"What does he do there?" I once asked an Englishman.

"Oh, he's just a bottle-washer," he replied. "He tells anecdotes in Allenby's mess."

Of the nature and contents of these anecdotes I heard much, and one of them I had the privilege of seeing in black-and-white: it was about my humble self.

It happened that shortly before the trouble with our American boys I wrote to Colonel Patterson, telling him that the lives both of the men of the Yishuv and of our men were being made a misery, and that this must inevitably lead to bitter and dangerous disillusionment. I sent a copy of the letter to General Allenby himself, drawing his attention to the unbridled incitement prevalent in the army and among the Arabs.

A week later this Jewish officer arrived in Tel Aviv and invited me to meet him at the house of Yechiel Weizmann, a brother of Dr. Weizmann. Yechiel Weizmann was present during our conversation.

"Allenby has your letter," said the captain. "He is almost ready to receive you and hear what you have to say. It depends on me. He asked me to meet you and to hear your complaints. Speak openly – we're Jews, after all."

I had no high opinion of him, especially after the Englishman's verdict; but, in common with the rest of the Yishuv, I had just as low an opinion of Allenby's ability at choosing confidantes. Who knows? – I thought – perhaps he is telling the truth. And I told him of my observations.

Several weeks later, a friend at G.H.Q. sent me a copy of the report on our conversation which the captain had submitted to the general. Of my "observations," not a single word appeared. About me personally, however – fire and brimstone. A heavily blackened portrait. The details concerning my character which I read there are hardly relevant. Only one point is worth mentioning: he had discovered that I was a "Bolshevik".... But I was told to go to Kantara to be demobilized; and in August, 1919, I was again a civilian.

Thus my personal memories of the Legion are ended. What happened later to the battalions I have already related. There remains but one chapter – in the nature of a father's speech at the graveside of his child; of a father who does not believe in graves and who believes that the child is not yet dead.

Chapter XIII
Conclusion

I must repeat what I said at the outset: I did not undertake to write a history of the Jewish Legion. In the first place, I have not the necessary material. The movement had its own history in each of the countries where it manifested itself: in Palestine, the United States, Canada, Argentina, Egypt. Trumpeldor's visit to Russia in Kerensky's time – a visit which all but resulted in the creation of a real Jewish Army – could not be disposed of in a chapter. And this refers only to the Legion "Movement." The Legion itself had a complex existence, of which I saw only a part. I was not in Gallipoli with the Zion Mule Corps, nor at Es Salt with Margolin's two companies. I could participate only in the internal life of my own battalion and not in that of the other two. And it was their internal life, particularly that of the Palestine volunteers, which was interesting. Of all these aspects of the movement and these experiences of the Legion, I have only documentary material and what I have is far from sufficient. And even the documents I have are scattered in the numerous "archives" which a wanderer like myself has to create for himself in each city where his life deposits him for a year or two. It would undoubtedly be desirable to compile a history of the Legion, but only people with the necessary means could achieve this. Perhaps the Americans, the richest among us, will one day undertake the task; I myself am unable to do so.

I have only recorded my personal memories, probably with all the faults which this kind of literature involves: subjective evaluations, sometimes an error in a date or a name, and too much of the "I." I need offer no explanations. Yet there is one explanation I do wish to make.

Have I written the truth? Yes, to my knowledge, I have written the whole truth. Without any bias, I have omitted a number of facts; for I do not believe that every fact is true in the fundamental sense. A great thing has a character – "features"; whatever is expressive of those features is part of the truth; whatever is in contradiction of that character is an accident, a scar, a rash. The most beautiful epochs of world history had their ugly stains. There are a thousand and one repulsive incidents that one can relate of the French Revolution, of Lincoln's Civil War, of Garibaldi's battles; and perhaps they should be related in a scientific history volume. But when one wishes to relate the essence of an episode, the beauty of which must today be universally affirmed, it is puerile to examine the mud – even though mud often gathers where people gather, it is puerile to mention, in a short survey of the French Revolution, that during the attack on the Bastille pickpockets were busily at work – even though it may be a fact. A healthy mind regards only what is important; and what is important is that which is expressive of the "features."

I must admit that, rereading what I had written, I often found myself laughing outright at myself: everything here appears much too smooth, too pretty. All good, all as brave as lions; anybody who assisted you appears like a perfect man. Have you forgotten the troubles, the humiliations, which you had to endure – and just from those heroes whom you have tendered so much praise? And when you mention with gratitude the assistance which you had from this or that Jewish leader, have you forgotten his ten stabs in the back, his twenty betrayals?

The memory is an autonomous mechanism, and a petty one. It

attracts tiny details, especially unpleasant ones, and does not like to detach itself from them. That is why we have been vouchsafed a controlling apparatus which we call "taste." There were many unpleasant details, bitterly unpleasant, often repulsive. But what does it matter? The Legion Movement and the Legion are part of Jewish history, and that part is a noble one, truly a noble one, composed of much suffering, of sacrifice, of goodwill, of sincere striving. That is what is important; the trifles which mar the smoothness of its features can interest only hostile gossips.

In saying this I humbly seek support from a great authority. Goethe once wrote of his life (in his autobiographic *Wahrheit und Dichtung*): "Not lies nor colored descriptions, but truth – yet truth cleaned of its offal." This is perhaps the only true form, the only worthy garment, in which the truth should appear before the world.

Yes, they were brave and good soldiers, efficient and healthy. Of course, I have not forgotten the rascal from New Jersey who habitually chewed gum on parade; and the "tailor" who was found sleeping at his post in No Man's Land; and especially that coward of a Londoner who deserted to the Turks eight days before the offensive. But Garibaldi, in the first days of his Sicilian campaign, was compelled to shoot three of his patriots for thieving. Does this affect the greatness of the thousand heroes with whom Italy's liberation began? Is 997 less than 1,000? In mathematics, yes; but not in history. They were "a thousand," and a thousand they remain in the eternal memory of their country and their people.

I have written the truth. The Jewish people may be proud of its five hundred mule drivers and of its five thousand fusiliers – of all of them, from Whitechapel, from Tel Aviv, New York, Montreal, Buenos Aires and Alexandria. They came from four continents, and one of them, Colonel Margolin, from the fifth, Australia. And they did their duty conscientiously and nobly for the Jewish future.

And proud may the Jewish people be, too, of those supporters and helpers who came to us from the Gentiles. Some of them bear great names in their own countries, some are less known, or unknown; but they were all of them great-hearted, noble souls – a good omen for the future, a proof that Israel is not altogether forsaken.

I have made several references to the significance of the Legion and I desire only to summarize what I have already written. Naturally, my evaluation is that of an interested party and therefore perhaps not altogether objective. The controversy on the Legion idea is far from ended. Those who do not want a new Legion will naturally underestimate the value of the old one, and vice versa. Perhaps I am part of the vice versa. Yet let not my attitude on the question be too lightly construed. When one is subjective through and through, one always tries to prove that one "won," "succeeded." I have not said that. I did not win: I dreamed of a great Jewish Army, not of five thousand men. But those five thousand did "succeed," the Legion itself did play a part, a decisive part, in the history of Zionism. That is my opinion; and as certain as I am of tomorrow's sunrise, so am I certain that posterity will make the same evaluation of the suffering and sacrifices of the Jewish Legion.

Its military significance was that which a few battalions can have in a great army. England could have liberated Palestine without us; but she liberated it with us, and, moreover, stationed us – as every expert will confirm – at one of the most difficult posts. It is not much, nor little; it is as much as it is. The ancient regiment of "Royal Fusiliers," whose name our battalions bore during the campaign, was through us given the right to inscribe on its flag – on which are already inscribed in golden letters, Crimea, India, Sudan, South Africa – a new name: Palestine. And the old British regiment is proud of its achievement. So are Patterson and Margolin, and I.

The significance of the Legion as a guardian of the peace in Palestine is quite a different matter. I have already said: as long as the five thousand kept guard over Palestine – even during a stormy period when they were on guard almost alone – there was peace. As soon as they disappeared, there broke out a series of pogroms: Jerusalem, Jaffa, Petah Tikva and again Jerusalem. There are people, opponents of the Legion, who, to their shame be it said, will look for excuses:

"It was not because of that..." Whether you love the Legion or not, you may not deprive those five thousand young Jews of the credit for saving God knows how many lives.

The moral value of the Legion must be clear to every thinking person, whether he is a pacifist or not. We all abhor war; it is nevertheless a fact that we obtained our official right to Palestine as the result of the war – that is, of great human sacrifices. It is difficult to imagine what our moral position would have been if people could throw the question in our faces: "Where were you? Why did none of you come forward and demand that you, as Jews, should also shed blood for your own country?" Today we have a reply: five thousand; and there would have been more, but for the procrastination of the British Government. It was this moral significance of the Legion which drew the sympathy of men like the then South African premier, Smuts, who, himself a pacifist, declared that it was one of the finest ideas he had heard of in his life.

But greatest of all was the political significance of the Legion. From day to day I saw the work of those men who immortalized their names in obtaining the Balfour Declaration for us; and they know how highly I value their work. And I am not forgetting that the efforts made in the years of the war were only a small part of the earlier strivings of the Jewish people for Palestine. For the Balfour Declaration we have to thank Herzl and Rothschild and Pinsker and Moses Hess; still more, the Bilu and those who followed them, the colonists, workers and teachers, from Ruhama in the south to Metulla in the north. Not to mention that which, more than anything else, helped to establish our claim: the Book which is holy to them as to us. Perhaps nine whole steps toward the goal, perhaps ninety-nine, were made before the war, and only the final step during the war. But that final step was a great one; and it is not just to forget that this step was a collective achievement – it is not just to remember only individuals, however great the credit due to them, and to forget five thousand. I say with the deep and cold conviction of an observer – speaking only of the short war period: half the Balfour Declaration belongs to the Legion. For the world is not an irresponsible organism; Balfour Declarations are not given to individuals. They can be given only to Movements. And how could the Zionist Movement express itself in those war years? It was broken and paralyzed, and was, by its nature, completely outside the narrow horizons of a warring world with its war governments. Only one manifestation of the Zionist will was able to break through on to this horizon, to show that Zionism was alive and prepared for sacrifice; to compel ministers, ambassadors and – most important of all – journalists, to treat the striving of the Jewish people for its country as a matter of urgent reality, as something which could not be postponed, which had to be given an immediate yes or no – and that was the Legion Movement.

The Jewish people did not thank those five thousand; they need no thanks. But in their inner consciousness there lives that feeling of pride to which I have given expression; the time will come when Jewish children will learn this truth together with their alphabets. And to each one of the five thousand I say what I once said to my "tailors," taking farewell of them at our last camp at Rishon: "Far away, in your home, you will one day read glorious news, of a free Jewish life in a free Jewish country – of factories and universities, of farms and theaters, perhaps of MPs and ministers. Then you will lose yourself in thought, and the paper will slip from your fingers; and there will come to your mind a picture of the Jordan Valley, of the desert by Rafah, of the hills of Ephraim by Abouein. Then you shall stand up, walk to the mirror, and look yourself proudly in the face. Jump to 'attention,' and salute yourself – for 'tis you who have made it."

*Jabotinsky's Place in the History of the Jewish People**

Benzion Netanyahu

Ladies and Gentlemen:

Let me begin by clearly defining the scope of my discussion; otherwise you might expect of me something which I cannot go into at this time. As we try to determine Jabotinsky's place in our history, we shall not seek to rate him among the various leaders who have influenced the course of our people throughout the ages. No one familiar with any significant part of Jabotinsky's accomplishments and performance would deny him a place of honor in our history – and this assessment must suffice for the present. A more precise evaluation should be left to the future – to a time when partisan passions subside

* Address delivered at the University of Haifa, the Rëuben Hecht Chair of Zionism, on January 13. 1981, marking the 100th anniversary of Jabotinsky's birth. Reprint from the Festschrift in honour of Dr. Rëuben Hecht on the occasion of his 70th birthday

and our historical vision broadens, so that we may judge Jabotinsky with fuller knowledge and greater objectivity. Accordingly, we shall not touch in this discussion upon Jabotinsky's innovations in *practical* politics, including his diplomatic and organizational activities, for the final outcome of his deeds in this field is still far from apparent, and we still lack the historical perspective needed for a proper evaluation. Today we shall limit our purview to Jabotinsky's contributions to our political thought – contributions which can be clearly discerned, defined, and duly assessed. However, we shall not deal here with some abstract, "pure" thought, detached from the reality of our history. Rather we shall consider Jabotinsky's political philosophy in the light of its relevance to Jewish life in the past two or three generations, and especially to our own life today. I believe it can help us evaluate our positions, understand our problems and determine our future course of action.

Now, what were Jabotinsky's innovations in the area of our political thought, and to what extent did his teaching bring about a transformation in our national values?

SURRENDER AND RESISTANCE IN JEWISH HISTORY

When we review Jabotinsky's writings and examine his ideas and his credo, we see that one supreme principle guided him throughout: resistance to subjugation. Along with this he advocated the creation of a multi-faceted force, including military force, to serve as the instrument of that resistance.

Few people today can see the novelty that all this represented. Is it not natural for any people to resist subjugation and forge the instruments of its defense? It is; but for the great majority of the Jewish people this was a dubious proposition until the turn of the century. That it has ceased to be so since that time testifies to the revolution that Jabotinsky brought about in our thinking on these matters. To properly evaluate this revolution, we must view our history from the standpoint of our capacity for active resistance to subjugation.

There is little need to point out that in antiquity we were a nation known for its superior capacity to "resist." We did not allow anyone to attack us, still less to endanger our existence, without reacting to such attempts with forceful opposition. It is enough to recall our determined stand against the ancient empires of the Near East and later our resistance to the Hellenistic and Roman Empires – a resistance expressed in recurring revolts over a period of 800 years (from the Hasmonean rebellion to the war against Heraclius in 614). Our capacity for resistance was retained also during our first few centuries of Exile; but it gradually diminished and was worn down until it virtually disappeared. Some historians consider the passing of the laws that prohibited Jews from bearing arms in Germany (probably already in the 12th century) as the beginning of degradation for the Jews in the West. And there may be much truth in this conception; for from that time on we were essentially transformed into what later became known as "protected Jews" – in practice, a group with no real power to defend its existence. True, in our other major center in Western Europe – i.e. in Spain – we still find in the twelfth century fortresses left in the exclusive control of Jews and defended by independent Jewish forces. We also find Jewish battalions taking part in the Christian campaigns against the Moors, and city Jews bearing arms up to the end of the fourteenth century. But in time these phenomena became increasingly scarce. In the great massacres of 1391, it is already difficult to discern any significant signs of what might be termed *forceful* resistance to the antisemitic bands that sought to destroy the Jews. In the middle of the fifteenth century, Alfonso de Cartagena, a Christian of Jewish origin, and son of the apostate Paul of Burgos, spoke of the Jews as known for their cowardice, unable to take part in military engagements, because they lacked the prerequisite qualities of character that make for a fighting man. The Jew, he said, has lost the warrior's courage which so distinguished his forefathers in ancient times; and in the context in which they were said, Cartagena's words ring true. They may serve to typify the Jews in the Diaspora, especially those of Eastern Europe, in which we lived for eight centuries. Far worse, the unwillingness to offer resistance, which had been regarded as a "curse" of the Diaspora, came gradually to be viewed as a *worthy* trait. An ideology which glorified this passivity also developed in due course; it even penetrated the ranks of the national movement, founded in the early 1880s.

In 1894, Bialik wrote in his poem, "At the Threshold of the House of Study": "Rather than be a lion among lions, I prefer to perish among the sheep." This, of course, was not Jabotinsky's position, nor was it the position of Political Zionism which appeared a few years after Bialik had written that famous poem. If we wish to summarize Jabotinsky's stand in this matter, as it is reflected in the *totality* of his writings, we may do so as follows: You may nurture the dream of eternal peace; you may strive for its advancement and realization; you may even try to behave like Isaiah's lion who "shall eat straw like the ox." But if you wish to see the day when such behavior becomes general, you must, in the meantime, be prepared for battle with the beasts of prey. To do so, you should use your teeth and nails, and if you have none, grow them. When Jabotinsky wrote his article, "Man is Wolf unto Man," he was thinking more of the relations between nations than between individuals. He understood that the realm of politics is one of *power conflicts,* in which the prevailing modes of behavior are those of *expansion and domination*. You either recognize this and act accordingly, or you suffer defeat. Whoever plays the game must learn its rules.

We can now appreciate the depth of the revolution which Jabotinsky, by his preaching of resistance, effected in our thinking, our moral values and the way we were to conceive our problem as a nation among the nations. *He taught resistance to a people who, for many generations, had lost the capacity and will to resist.*

RESISTANCE AND INDEPENDENCE

To understand still better the import of his teaching, we should remember that Jabotinsky viewed Resistance as a corollary of

Independence. To put it tersely, his thinking was this: By resisting attacks on your person and your rights, you resist attacks on your independence. To Jabotinsky, this equation remained valid also when the term *independence* was replaced with such terms as "freedom" or "self-respect," each of which constituted a cornerstone of his outlook – or, more precisely, of his philosophical view of both the real and ideal human society. We shall not go further into Jabotinsky's world outlook, and only point out that, in his political thinking, that outlook was expressed in firm opposition to the surrender of any right which the Jews possessed as individuals and as a nation. In such surrender he saw nothing commendable: no generosity, no forbearance, and no morality. In fact, he saw in it *immorality* – and of the worst sort. For if you surrender a right you possess, you have, in fact, submitted to robbery, he thought – even if you pretend to have acted nobly and to be above it all. By the same token, he did not consider such behavior wise or pragmatic, but precisely the opposite; for this is the nature of violent extortion: it gradually increases with its success. This explains Jabotinsky's stormy opposition to the symptoms of compromise and appeasement which he saw in the responses of the Zionist leadership to British Rule in Palestine *at its outset*. Jabotinsky's position at that time was similar to that of Nordau and Zangwill, those two great Zionist statesmen, who likewise criticized the policies of our leadership at that very time. We especially note Zangwill's slogan: *obsta principiis* (resist the beginnings) – that is, resist all bad things at their *outset*, for otherwise they will go from bad to worse. Jabotinsky, too, believed in this dictum. In his letter to Weizmann in 1919, he discusses the behavior of the British authorities in Palestine, which was antagonistic to the Jews and to the Balfour Declaration, and he rebukes Weizmann for not having offered forceful resistance to these "beginnings" – to the political foundations they were laying in Palestine. He wrote: "The fact that the Foreign Office is getting used to the idea that the Zionists will swallow and accept anything diminishes the value of our démarches. I am amazed that you do not see this."

And from these two principles which he upheld – resistance to subjugation and the demand for independence – stemmed both the activist-maximalist conception which became the essence of his political philosophy and his major contribution to Zionism – a contribution we find evident in three areas: the development of military values in Israel, the education towards political struggle, and the position to be taken on the Arab question.

PREREQUISITE FOR INDEPENDENCE

Let us begin with the military concept. Here, of course, we should indicate that the idea of the need for a Jewish military force to protect the resettlement and the future state could already be found in Herzl's writings. In *The Jewish State* he wrote: "We will have to establish an army of professionals, with the best modern equipment, to defend the state from within and from without." And in his speech to the *Hovevei Zion* in London in July, 1896, he said: "*I want only the type of settlement which we can defend with our own Jewish army.*" And this demand also appears in all the drafts of the charters which Herzl drew up. Moreover, he considered military service not only an honorable civic duty, but also one of the foremost principles upon which the state must be founded. This is why he agreed to admit to the Jewish state even recidivist criminals, provided they had served their sentences, but refused to accept army deserters from any country whatever. But these and other similar thoughts did not penetrate deeply into Zionist consciousness. Only a few grasped their full significance and linked these ideas with the overall worldview of the new Zionism.

Jabotinsky was one of these few. His approach to the idea of the army and the use of force was expressed most clearly. First, in the founding of the Hagana in Russia, then in creating the Jewish Legion, then in establishing the Hagana in Jerusalem, then in campaigning for the restoration of the Legion, then in advocating the abandonment of the *havlaga* policy, then in setting up the Irgun, and finally in supporting the armed revolt against British rule in Palestine. We see that in his military activism Jabotinsky far surpassed Herzl, although his views on these issues were grounded in solidly Herzlian concepts. But Jabotinsky went beyond Herzl also in another important matter: he realized that Herzl's ideas in this area had not taken root in Jewish thinking, and he understood that the time had come to introduce into Zionism not only an awareness of the *need* for an army, but also of the importance of *military values* as a positive element in a nation's life. He therefore spoke not only of a professional army for "defense from within and from without" (as Herzl wrote in *The Jewish State*), but also of educating our youth to the value of the military, so that the nation might face the hard battle which its national rebirth made inevitable. Accordingly, he found it necessary to explain that there is both good and bad militarism, just as there is both good and bad nationalism, and that there are certain lofty qualities and ideals which only a military education can impart.

Jabotinsky's position on this issue was not accepted by the majority of Zionists, who continued to attack him for his "militaristic" views. In fact, in this struggle for the new education of the young was revealed the vast gap between Jabotinsky and the Zionists of that generation, or, more correctly, the gap between that generation and the task which our history had set for it. It is difficult for us to comprehend today the bitter opposition which Jabotinsky encountered, for his demands now appear so elementary. At that time, however, they were not seen as elementary, but as revolutionary and, in any event, harmful. I shall cite here only one brief passage from an article by Medzini, a well-known journalist in his day, who was critical of Jabotinsky. "To tell the truth," he wrote, "a large part – perhaps a majority – of the Jewish community in Palestine – did not respond with over-enthusiasm to the idea of the Legion. The militaristic *Weltanschauung*, which is an inseparable part of the 'Caesarist' outlook of Jabotinsky and his disciples, *is remote and alien to many of us*." We, of course, find no "Caesarist" approach – today it would undoubtedly be called "imperialistic" – in Jabotinsky's writings. But what was then called *a militaristic outlook*, all that Jabotinsky wrote in praise of "militarism," without ignoring the negative characteristics it could acquire under certain conditions; all that he wrote in praise of the values it fosters and develops – discipline, collective action, mutual assistance, a spirit of self-sacrifice, daring and a capacity for acts of heroism; all these qualities in which he believed, all these concepts that his opponents labeled as "Jabotinsky's militarism," were adopted by the youth movements he created, and today they are the qualities which the army of Israel seeks to instill in all its members and in which the entire Jewish people takes pride.

THE THEORY OF "POLITICAL OFFENSIVE"

I now move on to Jabotinsky's contribution in the area of political struggle. It lay in his emphasis that the foremost means in this struggle is what he called *public pressure*; and to fully appreciate his views in this matter, we must clearly understand what he meant by that "pressure." In the first place, public pressure consisted, to his thinking, of airing a demand, a complaint, or an argument and standing firmly behind it; and its essence is that this demand or argument enjoy the support of public opinion. It is one of the ordinary means of power employed in struggles *within* and *among* nations. "For there is no friendship in politics," said Jabotinsky. "There is pressure. What tips the balance one way or another is not whether the ruler is good or bad, but the degree of pressure exerted by the subjects." Therefore:

> If pressure is exerted solely by our opponents, with no counter-pressure applied by us, then whatever is done in Palestine will be against us, even if the head of the government will be called Balfour, or Wedgwood, or even Theodor Herzl!... For no reformation in national conditions is attained without pressure and struggle. And whoever lacks the stamina, courage, ability, or desire to fight, will not be able to achieve even the smallest adjustment on our behalf, even if the government is made up of our most loyal friends. For the machine of government is above all a machine which submits to the laws of

> public pressure, just as a machine made of iron submits to the laws of physics.

Opposing this "pressure theory," many Zionist leaders claimed that it lacked substance in the case of the Jewish People, which could not support its claims by real power factors. Jabotinsky, however, denied this. He totally rejected what he called "the oldest refrain in the world" – the one which argues that "we are weak, small, helpless and powerless; we can be crushed with one finger, no one fears us, and so on."

"On the contrary," said Jabotinsky, "we are far closer to the truth than those who write hymns about our insignificance and weakness. If we amount to nothing, then let us not become involved in politics at all; let us not indulge in dreams of rights and territory; let us not struggle, but simply close up shop and go home. But the truth is that we do fight, we do forge ahead, step by step, simply because we are a world power. It may be difficult to recruit and concentrate this force, but it does exist and our enemies believe it."

Jabotinsky wrote these words in 1915, at the beginning of the First World War, and he returned to this theme, with ever-increasing emphasis, after the war was over. The theory of public pressure was a primary component of his overall political philosophy and constituted the essence of his critique against the Zionist leadership. Jabotinsky entertained no great hope that "diplomatic" negotiations between Jewish representatives and the British government would remove the obstacles from the path of Zionism *so long as such negotiations were not supported by favorable public pressure.* "This method," he said,

> may have been effective in the past, during the era of the Shtadlanim, when a conversation between a court Jew and the Austrian chancellor sufficed to save the whole Jewish community from an edict of exile. In those days, the chancellor represented the entire government, perhaps even the entire state. He did not have to consider the reactions of the press, Parliament,

> or public opinion. But today there are no such chancellors. Large-scale political activity in our time must appeal to the masses.... Look at England and you will see that such activities begin with a series of mass demonstrations. The interested masses act on their own, and ministers lend their ears not to delegations, but to the voice of the people.

At the Sixth Zionist Congress, Max Nordau said: "From the day the world was created to this very day, there have been only two ways to get anything: to take or to demand. To take, we cannot and do not wish; there remains therefore only the second way: to demand. It is amazing," added Nordau, "but absolutely true: before the advent of Zionism, we had actually not demanded. The change we introduced in this situation may appear to be minor, but it is actually very great. We have demanded." Political Zionism did indeed *demand*, addressing its demands both to the governments and to world public opinion. And it can be said that in this matter, too, Jabotinsky followed the path of Herzl and Nordau.

TRANSITION TO "CONFRONTATION"

Nevertheless, there was a difference between the activities that the latter carried out in this area and Jabotinsky's approach. For he advocated not only a public campaign aimed at acquiring friends for Zionism and defending it against false accusations. Such a campaign was indeed undertaken by the political Zionists and by Jabotinsky himself before and during the First World War. What Jabotinsky demanded *now*, however, was something else – something which he termed a "political offensive" – a sharply critical attack on British policy, directed not only at the British public but at world public opinion as a whole. This, of course, implied a *confrontation* with the British government along the entire international front, and here lay the main difference between Jabotinsky's stand and that of the Zionist leadership, which had done its utmost to remain in the realm of public information within the boundaries of a loyal opposition, defending established positions.

In April 1925, Jabotinsky said: "We should not distinguish between Zionism and the political offensive. We should prepare the ground for swaying *world* opinion and the governments, even hostile governments." And in August 1925, at the Fourteenth Zionist Congress, he declared:

> Both within and without this hall, we have been asked: Where will you find the strength to force the hand of the British Government? My answer is that Herzl, too, was asked: Where is your strength? You seek to transform the Land of Israel into the Jewish state, but where is your authority? And what will this man or that man say to this? But Herzl's answer was this: I cannot tell you how I will convince this or that party; perhaps political parties cannot be won over; but the world is not a political party and it can be convinced if we present it with logical demands. If this is the case, we need something which we term a "political offensive" in order to put our demands forth until they are met. For there are only two possibilities: we either can or cannot move the world to accept the truth. If we cannot, we will go down defeated, as we seek the impossible; if we can, however, let us try to move it.

Weizmann reacted. The confrontation advocated by Jabotinsky between the Zionist movement and the British government, the greatest power in the world at that time, appeared to him utter folly. In a declaration preceding the 1927 Zionist Congress, he wrote: "The point of departure of our future political activities must be the same as it was in the past: the maintenance of friendly relations with the Mandatory government and its representatives in Palestine. *There can be no second thoughts about this truth.*" Furthermore: "We cannot allow any part of the Zionist organization, nor any lone Zionist, to place obstacles in our path by holding irresponsible demonstrations in Jerusalem, London or anywhere else." Those who understood knew, of course, to which methods he referred and to which "lone Zionist" he alluded. But not all Zionists fully agreed with this opinion of Weizmann. Even Mr. Medzini, Weizmann's sworn defender, was forced to admit that, on this issue, Jabotinsky was correct "to a certain extent" in criticizing existing methods. "There is no doubt," said Medzini, "that the leaders of the organization committed a grave error in not considering it vital to carry on large-scale political propaganda in England. As a result, the impression has now been created there that the Jews are completely satisfied with all that is being done by the British authorities and that only the Arabs protest and object to the government's activities." It is evident that Medzini failed to note the thrust of Jabotinsky's thinking, that he limited his concurrence solely to the area of appeal to England. We have already stressed that Jabotinsky referred not only to the struggle within England, but also to the contest on the *international* front. But at this point something else should be added. Jabotinsky wrote: "We wish to persuade public opinion in England and all other countries and to prove the *justice* of our claims. We believe that a truth presented to the civilized world and defended with full self-respect, will ultimately prove victorious."

Today, as the political world has changed so much from its pre-war condition, many, in all likelihood, will doubt the practical value of this prognosis. Nowadays, as we see justice trampled underfoot even in places where once it used to flourish, it is most difficult to maintain faith in the notion that the truth "will ultimately prove victorious." Nevertheless, one thing cannot be denied even in these dismal times: all who appeal to public opinion – be their claims the most wicked imaginable – do so in the name of "justice." For otherwise it is impossible to appeal to public opinion at all. And what must be indicated, to begin with, is that Jabotinsky had complete faith in the *full and total justice of our claims*. Without such absolute faith, he saw neither basis nor hope for our struggle. And it should be remembered that also from this standpoint – i.e. the moral standpoint – he demanded not only *defense* of our positions, but also, and especially, an all-out *offensive,* a frontal assault on enemy positions with no room for compromise or concession. Without such an attack, which would reestablish our valid, absolute and unquestionable right to the Land of Israel, we could not be victorious in this battle, he thought. And he further believed that this offensive was important not only for the conquest of public opinion, and not only for our friends and allies around the world, but also for ourselves and our children; because *as Jews we are committed to the moral thesis,* and without being certain that we are fighting for a just cause, we will not be able to devote to this struggle all the dedication and resolution which are essential to victory.

Only on one occasion in the history of Zionism could Jabotinsky's method of political offensive prove its effectiveness in actual test. This was at the beginning of the Second World War, when two delegations representing Jabotinsky's movement – one from the New Zionist Organization and the other from the Irgun – worked in the United States. Both these delegations stormed American public opinion to get its support for Zionist objectives. The results of their activities were quickly seen: widespread sympathy for the Zionist aims was created in the American public, including both Jews and non-Jews. Then, with the help of friendly elements in the Zionist organization of America, the leadership of that organization was taken over by people who favored Jabotinsky's methods. Thus a vast front was created which virtually forced the U.S. government to support the Zionist demands. Obviously, this movement alone, had it not been accompanied by the armed revolt on the part of our underground forces in Palestine, would not have been able to bring about the establishment of a Jewish state. But I also believe that this revolt alone, had it remained limited to this corner of the world, and not been used as it was for recruitment of public opinion in the United States, would likewise not have led to the results attained – that is, to the establishment of the State of Israel.

THE ARAB PROBLEM

I now come to the third aspect of Jabotinsky's contribution to our political thinking – his stand regarding the Arab question. It is commonly believed that this problem – i.e. the Arab problem – was correctly perceived by those who were called "practical Zionists," or by those who had spoken of Arab-Jewish rapprochement since the beginning of the British Mandatory period. Herzl and his colleagues, we are told, did not take the Arab question into consideration. Yet nothing could be further from the truth than this popular misconception. Anyone familiar with Herzl's writings knows that he was *certain* of the coming of a consolidated resistance by the indigenous population to the settlement of Jews in Palestine, once it passed a certain point, and especially if the authorities viewed it with disfavor. Hence he objected to the *Hovevei Zion* program and demanded a contract with international guarantees ensuring proper defense for the settlers and the unhampered progress of the settlement. I have already written on this matter long ago and will not linger on it here. Regarding Nordau and Zangwill, it is enough to read their articles and speeches from 1919 on to appreciate the gravity and concern with which they viewed the danger of Arab opposition. Indeed, their political recommendations and their criticism of both British and Zionist policies at the time were rooted in this concern. No one, however, preceded or surpassed Jabotinsky in his thorough grasp of the overall meaning of the Arab problem during the period following the British conquest. Jabotinsky noticed the *birth* of Arab resistance, which was nurtured and supported by the British policy. He also understood that it could quickly develop into an independent force, hardened to an extent which would make it difficult to restrain, for he discerned the *natural* roots of this resistance, as did Herzl and Nordau, realizing that therein lay the core of the problem. To be sure, he believed that the flames of this movement *could* be extinguished at the outset, and that had this been done, they would have disappeared; but they were *not* extinguished; they were rather fanned; and he realized how dangerous this flare-up might become. Therefore, as early as 1919 he saw an urgent need for opposing the British policy that encouraged the Arabs towards hostile acts against the Jews. This was also the reason for his severe criticism of the Zionist leadership which did not grasp the full nature of British activity and did not oppose it with appropriate resolve. In June 1920, in his letter to the Jewish community in Palestine from the Acre prison, he wrote:

> Weizmann is a diplomatic genius, but he never understood the political situation in Palestine. He never realized the decisive value of all that is being done here as a precedent. During all the years of this extended pogrom, he stifled our pent-up protests, while our enemies' audacity grew stronger and firmer and struck deep roots, whereupon we became open prey in their eyes. Last Passover [during the Passover pogrom in Jerusalem], he saw with his own eyes the results of this policy. Yet even after this debacle he has learned nothing and forgotten nothing, continuing his politics of blindness and leading us to even greater ruin.

As Arab resistance consolidated more and more, and as it developed with British support, it became a phenomenon demanding special treatment. And before we touch further on this point, we ought to make it clear, it seems to us, that Jabotinsky did not hate the Arabs, nor did he belittle them. What he wrote in his poem: "There [namely in Palestine], flourishing in plenty and joy, will dwell Arabia's son, the son of Nazareth and my own son," undoubtedly represented his heart's desire. Nevertheless, he did not believe that the "plenty and joy" that the Zionist enterprise could offer to the Arabs would serve as sufficient inducement for them to abandon their desire to drive us from the land. Hence he dismissed as a "juvenile illusion" the hope that the Arabs would agree to the realization of Zionism in return for the cultural and economic advantages that Zionism could assure them. And in contrast to the various peace plans and the preaching for reconciliation which were then flooding the Jewish press, Jabotinsky wrote:

> The delusion entertained by these Arabophiles of ours originates in some disparagement of the Arab people. According to these Arab-lovers, the Arab people appears to be nothing but a greedy rabble, ready to sell out its patriotism in exchange for a well-developed railway system. This view is without foundation: individual Arabs may, of course, be bribed, but this does not mean that the Arabs of Palestine in general are prepared to sell out that patriotic zeal which even the Papuans refuse to relinquish. Every indigenous people will fight against settlers [from the outside] so long as there exists even a glimmer of hope for them to eliminate the alien settlement. This is how the Arabs of Palestine have behaved up until now, and this is how they will go on behaving, so long as they retain a spark of hope to prevent the transformation of Palestine into the Land of Israel.

And, on another occasion, he wrote with similar emphasis:

> So long as the Arabs have even a glimmer of hope of getting rid of us, neither pleasant words nor attractive promises will induce them to abandon this hope. This is precisely because they are not a rabble, but a nation. And a living nation will concede on such fateful issues as these only when there is no hope left of changing the situation and when all chinks in the iron wall have been sealed.

What, then, is the answer to the Arab question? The "iron wall" – that is, a strong military and political force which will ultimately convince the Arabs that it is impossible for them to drive us out. The existence of an iron wall does not preclude attacks upon it, or attempts to break it down. In 1885, Nordau stated as a general condition, without relating it specifically to the situation in Palestine: "When two nations fight over the same land, the problem can be solved only by the sword." And in 1926, when tranquility prevailed in Palestine, Jabotinsky wrote:

"I admit that there are moments when I dream of a Jewish-Arab agreement regarding the Land of Israel. This occurs during moments of fatigue, when a man is weary of bearing it all." Actually, he did not believe that there was any possibility for this dream to be realized; therefore, he summed up: "I fear that we shall attain the Land of Israel only through battle."

Now, the question may be asked whether Jabotinsky's ideas were corroborated by contemporary political reality. The answer is before us. The Arabs received all the countries they had dreamed of; they received also most of the Land of Israel; and they have a Palestinian state which occupies some 75% of the area of Mandatory Palestine. Yet they want *all* of Palestine, from one end to the other. To the extent we established ourselves in our land, we did so through war, just as Jabotinsky had foreseen. But Arab resistance still continues. Not only has it failed to diminish; it has increased, acquiring global dimensions, commensurate with the influence the Arabs now wield and the significance of the areas they control. They are also supported by most of the great powers and a vast majority of the world's nations. According to Jabotinsky, their resistance will not cease so long as they maintain even a "glimmer of hope" of eliminating our presence here. And who will deny that they have such a glimmer – and indeed much more than a "glimmer" only? Thus, there is no possibility of peace with the Arabs – that is, a *true* peace – at this time, for they have not yet been convinced that it is impossible to destroy us or drive us into the sea.

SUMMARY AND CONCLUSION: THE TEST OF TIME

To sum up, I believe that in these three areas – in the promotion of military values, in stressing the importance of "public pressure," and in the comprehension of the Arab question – Jabotinsky made his greatest contributions to determining the political course of Zionism. I have shown that in fashioning his policies in all these issues, Jabotinsky started from key positions of political Zionism, but went far beyond them. He created operational methods which, whether we agree with them or not, are understood far better in our day than they were during the time he struggled so hard for their promulgation. The appreciation of military values, which so many condemned in his day, has now become a reigning principle not only in Israel, but throughout the world. At the time when Jabotinsky began to argue for this concept, many believed that the days of the Messiah were drawing nigh, that the world was progressing toward general disarmament, international peace and universal brotherhood. Today we know that this is not so, or that the chances for it are slim indeed. Moreover, in addition to the standard risks, the risks of wars we call "conventional," there is the danger of nuclear war which becomes increasingly realistic. Who would deny today that military education and the attendant values it develops and nurtures – just as Jabotinsky perceived and taught – constitute a primary factor in our lives?

And such is also the case regarding the methods we should pursue in our political struggle. The "public pressure" which Jabotinsky advocated was, of course, already much in use in the politics of his time. Its importance, however, increased significantly following the First World War, as the principles of democracy spread through Europe and reached the borders of Soviet Russia. Under such conditions, Jabotinsky thought, public opinion would be more likely than ever to influence nations and governments – and in this he was doubtlessly right. But what happened later, following the entry of the United States into the Second World War and into the international political arena – and especially what happened *after* that war – raised the importance of public opinion to a level hitherto unknown in history, thus further corroborating Jabotinsky's views. For public opinion in the United States is able, more than any other factor, to determine and change policies, and even to establish and bring down governments; and today all nations and countries compete for the use or control of this factor. Thus, just as in the case of the *military* education, Jabotinsky's views regarding *public opinion* – or what he termed the political offensive – appear today to be even more correct, valid and realistic than they ever were in the past.

And little need be said regarding the Arab question. It is obvious that Jabotinsky saw the Arab attitude as far more intransigent and far less amenable to compromise and rapprochement than did many others of his generation. It is also clear that the only power preventing our destruction today is the "iron wall" which we set up with our own strength. Who would dare surrender this iron wall? Who would dare recommend that it be weakened? True, this is not the wall Jabotinsky envisioned, for he was thinking of a *political* wall no less than of a military one, and understood what we have learned only later from bitter experience: that military victory is incomplete unless protected by political victory, and political victory is incomplete unless defended by public opinion.

In all these areas, Jabotinsky showed a higher degree of political acumen, a greater sense of reality and a stronger grasp of the global historical processes than any other Jewish leader. It may be said that his theories and activities removed us from the idyllic, naive and provincial world in which Zionism had dallied during the Mandate, forcing us out into the real and harsh world of our own times, teaching us to look at it with our eyes wide open. In this respect, Jabotinsky, who in his values and ideals was essentially a nineteenth-century man, was in fact the person who removed us from that era and placed us right down in the hub of the twentieth century – this terrible century in which we live – providing us with the direction, compass and navigational rules needed to guide our ship of state through the storms of time.

These were Jabotinsky's principal contributions to our national political thought, and I might have ended my remarks here, had I not felt the need to comment on one other important matter. It does not relate to our national *positions*, but to the *method* by which they are determined – that is, to the way in which we draw the conclusions on which depend our national policies. I refer to the ability to prognosticate developments – and by this I mean primarily political developments – in which Jabotinsky distinguished himself to a very high degree. In this sphere, too, we can appreciate Jabotinsky only by comparing his personal achievements to our people's achievements throughout its history. And here again we can note a sharp line that divides our history into two great epochs: our nation, which in ancient times produced so many people who were capable of foreseeing coming events, was transformed in its Exile into a nation that appeared to have been stricken with blindness in this regard. In none of the periods of our life in the Diaspora, up to the start of the struggle for emancipation, do we find an understanding of things as they develop, still less of things that are about to happen. We did not foresee the catastrophes that befell us (such as the Exile from Spain, for instance) even a short time before they occurred, and therefore they always seemed to our ancestors as thunders out of a clear sky. It may indeed be said that during this period, "prophecy vanished from Israel."

During the period of the struggle for emancipation, we can find the first attempts in our midst to forge an overall national policy through predictions of political or social developments. Actually, however, all these attempts revolved on one prognosis: The world is "progressing" towards human equality and our people's problem will likewise be solved in the course of this irreversible process. This view guided the activities of individuals like Gabriel Riesser, among others. In contrast, as is known, our national movement arrived, since Hess, at the opposite conclusion: granted that mankind is progressing towards equality (of one form or another), this progress alone will not do away with the plague of antisemitism. As in the case of the view it opposed, this determination, too, led to far-reaching conclusions. But here again there was only one prognosis, which clearly did not suffice for the ramified needs of our emerging national movement. One may say that a *systematic* prognostication which could aid our nation in mapping out its path began only with Political Zionism. It was especially prominent in the activities of Herzl, who considered it a requirement of the highest order. For, far better than others, Herzl understood that no national policies can be set without attempts to diagnose the future and that no *correct* policies can be shaped without an accurate forecast of events.

This forecast of the future of which we speak is not at all a matter related to mysticism. It is not a product of supernatural powers, but something within the compass of human abilities. In fact, to assess the future in this context is merely to understand the *present* processes, to sense their direction, assess their influences and evaluate the results of developing conflicts. Once you perceive these processes properly, you already see the edge of the future. This is basically what it amounts to, but of course it is not a simple matter. Not in vain did our Sages state: "Wise is he who can foresee the future."

Jabotinsky, too, considered "seeing the future" as something which is within the sphere of "wisdom" – that is, something which is within our powers. He saw in it, moreover, the essence of statesmanship, and even of public guidance generally (and not in vain did he define, on one occasion, the Prophets of Israel as "publicists"). His writings are replete with historical observations on which he based his prognoses, the great majority of which have come true; and his principal method in arriving at his forecasts included careful analysis of the related data, as well as a logical, meticulous assessment of the probable, possible and impossible alike. But beyond these analytical skills, Jabotinsky was assisted in this matter by something else which must be pointed out. As in all areas of human inquiry, in this area, too, we sometimes attain a clear perception of the object of our inquiry through a special *flash*, an intuitive insight which clarifies both the problem and its solution as if in one stroke. No greatness may be achieved in any field without "flashes" of this sort. And Jabotinsky was blessed with such inspirations to a very large degree.

Let me touch on one important issue that will illustrate what I have just said. Zionist thinking before Herzl assumed that antisemitism would not disappear, or diminish, under the influence of the hopeful, dual processes of progress and emancipation. But, on the other hand, it did not discern that antisemitism was approaching peaks unlike anything it had reached before. In contrast, Herzl foresaw this development. Noting the driving force of modern antisemitism and its special ideological foundations, Herzl concluded, without any reservations, that antisemitism would continue to expand and intensify until it could attain its objective – the liquidation of European Jewry. He described this liquidation in clear terms and saw the solution in a rapid Exodus similar to what Jabotinsky perceived a few decades later.

Undoubtedly, Herzl's view of antisemitism and some of his ideas about its final goal imprinted themselves on Jabotinsky's mind and guided much of his thinking. In any case, soon after Hitler's rise to power, Jabotinsky was convinced that the time of the *catastrophe*, so repeatedly predicted in Herzl's writings, was drawing near. He reached this conclusion, just as Herzl did before him, not out of a sudden nightmarish seizure, or a psychosis of fear, or an eschatological vision, but out of a rational analysis of the facts as he saw them in clear and sober perspective. "I warn you, dear readers," he wrote in May 1939, "of the natural tendency to take comfort in the thought that not all expected outcomes materialize; that they may not materialize at all; that my conclusions are based only on human logic and life isn't always logical. I am warning you, because where Jewish fortunes are concerned, life is always logical, and every stone will shatter glass, and every spark will light a conflagration."

With this clear view of the future of the Jews within the framework of the European conditions, he wrote as early as 1935: "A nation of many millions, in its full powers and talents, is rolling downhill to the abyss of disaster, and people whisper in its ears that it should console itself with a trickle of *Aliya* instead of a massive *Exodus*" (the same term used by Herzl). And after repeated warnings on the danger of annihilation threatening European Jewry, he wrote in January 1939:

> To tell the truth, I sometimes fear that we've passed the eleventh hour. The clock may have already struck twelve – i.e., it is midnight, i.e., the end. But we must shake off this fear. Let it be only the eleventh hour. We can still look around us, we

> can still make a quick calculus; perhaps we can still find in the burning horizon a place which the flames have yet to reach, and perhaps we'll try to save ourselves.

Once again, in June 1939, he stressed the approach of the "zero hour," the hour of the *great destruction,* as he called it ("d-e-s-t-r-u-c-t-i-o-n, learn this word by heart," he wrote). Thus we have here a series of predictions, recurring with growing frequency, all saying one thing: the "doom," the "end," the "catastrophe." In light of this conviction, it was clear to Jabotinsky that the times called for an outstanding action, some audacious, unprecedented effort to break through the iron barrier that prevented the mass rescue. Only when we bear this in mind can we understand the plan Jabotinsky put forth in August 1939 – to organize a revolt against the British in Palestine, with himself personally in the lead, to take over the control of the country, even if for a brief period – a revolt that was meant to break out in October 1939.

How strange that, in view of this, there are still among us writers and researchers who keep sounding the old refrain that *no one* had predicted the holocaust. Of course: no one had predicted the exact time, place and circumstances in which the holocaust was to occur. But there was *someone* who realized that the necessary conditions – the social and moral conditions for its occurrence – had been fully prepared, and there was someone who warned again and again of its outbreak in the very near future. That "someone" was Jabotinsky, whose warnings sounded then like a voice crying in the wilderness.

I will not dwell further on this point – there is no need. But it's hard for me to end my comments on this subject without citing the following passage. It is an excerpt from Jabotinsky's speech in Warsaw on the Ninth of Av, 1938. It may serve to set the record straight on the matter in question:

> For three years I have been imploring you, Jews of Poland, the crown of world Jewry, appealing to you, warning you unceasingly that the catastrophe is nigh. My hair has turned white and

> I have grown old over these years, for my heart is bleeding that you, dear brothers and sisters, do not see the volcano which will soon begin to spew forth its fires of destruction. I see a horrible vision. Time is growing short for you to be spared. I know you cannot see it, for you are troubled and confused by everyday concerns.... Listen to my words at this, the twelfth hour. For God's sake: let everyone save himself, so long as there is time to do so, for time is running short.
>
> And I want to say something else to you on this day, the Ninth of Av: Those who will succeed in escaping the catastrophe will live to experience a festive moment of great Jewish joy – the rebirth and establishment of the Jewish state! I do not know whether I myself will live to see it – but my son will! I am certain of this, just as I am certain that the sun will rise tomorrow morning. I believe in it with all my heart.

Anyone who could speak *thus* one year before the beginning of the Holocaust, ten years before the founding of the State of Israel, was no ordinary political forecaster. *The light of prophecy shone upon him* – something of the light that shone upon that prophet of Israel who said: "The heavens were opened and I saw visions of God."

Glossary

A

Ashkenazi – Jew of Occidental (German, Polish, Russian) origin.

B

Betar, Brit Trumpeldor – Zionist youth organization founded by V. Jabotinsky.

Bilu – first groups of Jewish youth in Russia who proceeded, starting 1882, to Palestine to establish agricultural settlements.

"Black Hundred" (*Tchernaya sotnya*) – reactionary antisemitic wing in Russian politics after 1905, during the reign of Czar Nicholas II.

C

Haluka Jews – indigent Jews in Palestine who live on funds provided by philanthropic organizations from abroad.

D

"*Davar*" – Palestine Hebrew daily, organ of the labor movement.

Duma – Parliament in Czarist Russia.

G

Galut (Diaspora, dispersion) – comprises all countries outside of Palestine.

Ger (plural, gerim) – a Gentile convert to Judaism.

Goy – non-Jew, Gentile.

Grusinian – same as Georgian.

"*Gueules cassées*" ("broken pans") – maimed war veterans in France.

H

Hagana – Jewish self-defense organization in Palestine.

Hasidim – followers of a Jewish religious sect.

Hatikva – Zionist national anthem.

Hehalutz – organization of pioneers in Palestine.

Heder – Jewish religious school.

Hibbat Zion – Zionist movement which originated among Russian Jewry prior to the formation of the Zionist Organization.

"*Hob ich ihm in dr'erd*" (Yiddish) – "The devil take him!"

K

Keren Hayesod – Zionist Fund which raises on an international scale contributions for the colonization and rebuilding of Palestine.

Kevutza – name of the collectivist agricultural colonies, established by Jews in Palestine.

Kosher – food prepared in conformity with Jewish ritual prescriptions.

L

Lehavdil – Hebrew expression used to discriminate between sacred and profane, clean and unclean, etc.

M

Magen David (Shield of David, also known as "Solomon's seal") – Hebrew symbol made up of two interlaced triangles.

Menora – seven-branch candelabrum which plays an important role in Hebrew national and religious symbolism.

Mizrahi – Orthodox wing of the Zionist movement.

P

Plehve – Russian minister, famous for his reactionary and antisemitic policy.

Poale Zion – one of the Labor parties in Zionism.

R

Red Magen David – Hebrew equivalent of the Red Cross.

S

Sephardi – Jew of Oriental Spanish origin.

Shalom – Hebrew greeting.

Shehecheyanu (Lord ... who has perpetuated us to this day) – Hebrew thanksgiving prayer.

Shohet – slaughterer authorized to slaughter cattle and poultry according to the Jewish ritual.

T

Tel Hai – a Hebrew colony in Galilee; here, in 1920, Trumpeldor died a hero's death, defending the colony with a handful of men and women against overwhelming hordes of Bedouin.

Tsarevitch – crown prince in Russia.

Y

Yishuv – the Hebrew population of Palestine.

Index

The Toby Press publishes fine writing
on subjects of Israel and Jewish interest.
For more information, visit www.tobypress.com